W9-BFB-067

Sent

Reflections for Christians on Mission

Tim Way

Copyright © 2017 Tim Way

All rights reserved.

ISBN-13: 978-1977504524

Unless otherwise indicated, all Scripture quotations are from THE
HOLY BIBLE, NEW INTERNATIONAL VERSION®, NIV®
Copyright © 1973, 1978, 1984, 2011 by Biblica, Inc.® Used by
permission. All rights reserved worldwide.

Scripture quotations marked (NLT) are taken from the Holy Bible,
New Living Translation, copyright © 1996, 2004, 2007 by Tyndale
House Foundation. Used by permission of Tyndale House
Publishers, Inc., Carol Stream, Illinois 60188. All rights reserved.

Scripture quotations marked (MSG) are taken from *The Message*.
Copyright © 1993, 1994, 1995, 1996, 2000, 2001, 2002. Used by
permission of NavPress Publishing Group.

Scripture quotations marked (NASB) are taken from NEW
AMERICAN STANDARD BIBLE®, Copyright ©
1960,1962,1963,1968,1971,1972,1973,1975,1977,1995 by The
Lockman Foundation. Used by permission.

Scripture quotations marked (NCV) are taken from New Century
Version®. Copyright © 2005 by Thomas Nelson. Used by
permission. All rights reserved.

Photo credit (back cover): Kevin Trujillo. www.kevinjtru.com

DEDICATION

I dedicate this book to Jesus with the prayer that it will be for His glory and His Kingdom.

Under Jesus, I dedicate this to Jill, my wife and co-worker in the Gospel. All I have written comes out of our shared life of mission and family and walking with Jesus.

Finally, I dedicate this to the memory of my friend and brother Godfrey Kayita, who passed from this life months before I wrote the first pages. I miss you.

CONTENTS

Gratitude i

A Letter vi

1   The Father 1

2   Beautiful Waste 7

3   The Root Command 12

4   Fruitful Ministry 19

5   Intercession 24

6   What's So Great About the Gospel? 29

7   Gospel Story 35

8   Winning the Lost 40

9   The Poor: *What Are We to Do?* 46

10 The Simulator 55

11 Lonely Places 63

12 Emily's Story 70

13 War of the Spirit 74

14 Darkness, Demons, and Glory 79

15 Together............................... 86

16 Thursday Night Light Story...................... 91

17 TNL Lessons............................. 96

18 The Deal-Changer................................. 102

19 The Prize.................................. 107

20 Knowing Jesus 113

21 And Making Him Known.......................... 119

22 All For Jesus............................. 123

23 Passions.................................... 127

24 Encounter and Engage 131

25 Be Weak.................................. 136

26 Plod 142

27 God's Family............................... 148

28 Family or Mission? 157

29 To Narnia and Back 165

30 Your Call 171

31 What About Your Life?............................ 179

GRATITUDE

This book has been bouncing around in the dubious space between my ears for a decade, taking up space and making a general nuisance of itself. Over the past couple of years, it has grown and taken up more and more room, much like the clutter of boxes and other debris in my garage. In recent months, I find that I continually bump into it when trying to apply my limited brain power to other matters. Now I am on the cusp of sending it on its way, and I wonder if I'm going to miss it. It has been my private companion for so long. I also wonder what it will be like to share it with others. It's scary and exhilarating. In any case, I must. It's no masterpiece, but it is very personal. It's me to the core.

I am very grateful to have had the experience of living with and writing this simple collection of reflections. There are so many people to whom I am profoundly indebted. As I reflect on how this has become a reality, I realize it is because Jesus worked through a small army of people to push me on my way.

First, I must say thank you to my wife Jill. There's more to express than this medium will allow, so here I simply say thank you and I love you. Your encouragement, support, wisdom, and determined believing in me keep me going. To our five kids: Rebekah, Peter, Nathan, Philip, and Hannah. Thank you for all your encouragement and support and allowing me the hours to put into this dream. I love you and am proud of you and simply can't say enough. You are the best.

i

I would never have even started this if not for Debbie Tietsort of Believers World Outreach. Thank you for believing in me and supporting me. Thank you for commissioning me to develop a simple equipping tool for short-term mission trips. I didn't know that would become this, but I'm really thankful. Thank you also for trusting me to serve BWO teams in Uganda, and for being a friend.

To the Tulsa Boiler Room family: I don't know how to express my love and gratitude and respect for you all. You have helped to shape me and have supported me and stuck with me. You deserve credit for whatever good is in this book. You truly have become family to me, and you mean more to me than I could tell you. You help me to know Jesus more deeply, and you are true partners in the Gospel.

To my co-workers and brothers in Uganda – Tushabe, Israel, Kintu, and Kasozi: For nearly two decades we have labored together, and you have taught me about life and ministry and radically following Jesus. Thank you.

Thank you Jesse, Karissa, and James for allowing me to tell a bit of your story. More than that, thank you for tutoring me in relational ministry to the poor, and for giving me the opportunity to come alongside you and work together in the Kingdom. TNL has become one of the most significant parts of my life, and I am so grateful to you all and your unfailing friendship. Thank you to all the other leaders and team members over the years who have sustained and grown this work, and for whose friendship I am overwhelmingly grateful. At the risk of not being sufficiently thorough, I simply must mention by name a few whose years of service and friendship continue to shape and lift me: Rachel and Katie, Travis, Jeff, James Patrick, Justin, Janae, Micah, and Sarah. I also must add ORU's dream team of outreach leaders: Molly, Jaci, Aaron, and Josh. You all are simply amazing. And of course, Paul and Debbie: thank you for including me in the dream of the Merchant. Partnering with you in this endeavor is one of the best things ever. Your relentless compassion and zeal for the work of Jesus continue to stir me.

Thank you, Emily, for allowing me to share your story in these pages, and even more for inviting me to actually step into it with you in a small way. Your work is significant, and has deeply impacted me and many others. Your courage and compassion and faith inspire me. Thank you also to all who have made the trek to Reynosa with Emily at one time or other, and added your prayers and love to the work there.

Tyler, Jesse, and Seth. Thank you for everything. As you well know, the Tulsa Boiler Room would not have come to be without your leap of faith. I'm so grateful. Tyler, we've journeyed together across the States, as well as to the UK, Mexico, and Africa. Thanks for dreaming with me all those years ago, and for working and sacrificing to see those dreams come to reality. I'm glad we're still friends. Jesse, not only for TNL and the Boiler Room, but for a valued friendship that has survived the years, I'm really grateful. Seth, for your zealous determination to pursue Jesus and for all the ways you have shaped our community, and for your committed friendship, thank you.

Of course, I am ridiculously indebted to our Tulsa Boiler Room leaders: Jill, James, Katie, Oliver, Heidi, John, Nicole,

Micah, and Sarah: Your friendship in the journey is one of the great wonders of my life. I'm not giving you the space here that you deserve, but I hope you each know how I love you and deeply appreciate you. I am also so grateful to all of our past leaders, who have each profoundly impacted our community, and me personally: Caleb, Heather, Arvell, Kiem, Karissa, Laura, Rachel, Jeremiah, Alana, and Emily.

Thank you to the mission directors at Oral Roberts University over the past ten years or so who have graciously allowed me to participate in the equipping and receiving of short-term missionaries and local outreach teams. I'm thinking of Tammy Schneider, Bobby Parks, and now Augustine Mendoza. I've learned so much from you and from the experience of working with your students, and I so appreciate the friendships with each of you that have developed to my benefit.

The living author and preacher who has probably influenced me more than any other is Floyd McClung. As I write this, Floyd is in a rehab hospital in Cape Town, South Africa, fighting simply to live another day. Along with his wife Sally, he has taught and inspired and shaped me from afar. The few times I've had the privilege of face-to-face encounters have been highlights in my life. My prayers and sincerest gratitude are with you.

Thank you to my extended family and co-workers in the 24-7 Prayer Movement and Believers Church. I'm so honored to be part of this wild and wonderful… thing. Although this is a large tribe, I must single out Roger Nix for his unceasing support and encouragement over the past fifteen years or so. I love and appreciate you. Your friendship means a lot to me.

Last but not least, thank you to those who have read this manuscript and offered feedback, especially Rachelle Rummage and Christi Sleiman. Your responses and thoughtful questions gave me encouragement when I needed it most.

And thank you especially to Bob Burch for the hours and hours you gave to reading and editing and correcting and trying to shape my often incoherent thoughts into something people could actually follow. I seriously don't know what I would have done without you. Sorry for all the exasperating use of fragments. And, incorrect use of commas. And lists. ;)

A LETTER TO YOU

Dear Reader,

As I put the finishing touches on this little book, I am praying for you. I pray that somehow in these pages you will hear the calling of the Spirit of God. I pray that, like the early disciples on the shores of the Sea of Galilee, you will hear the voice of Jesus calling you to come and follow. The world in which we live and hope and dream and struggle has a way of drowning out that voice. May it not be so with us.

I've written this with some specific situations in mind. First, I am addressing people going on short-term mission trips. I love it that you're going in His Name to do His work. I hope you will find these simple reflections deeply challenging. I also hope they will bring you refreshment and hope as you give of yourself each day. Secondly, I am thinking about folks who participate in regular outreaches, endeavoring to demonstrate the love of Jesus in your own community. I am so grateful for your service and witness for Jesus. I pray this will help in some small way.

I realize that these are two pretty specific scenarios. One person who read this manuscript kindly suggested I write a book of devotionals "just for life." My response was that this is what I have done. The life of a follower of Jesus is a life of mission and outreach. The devotionals contained here are pretty much the ones I would include in a collection "just for life." So, maybe you have picked up this book even though you are not on a missions trip, and neither are you part of an organized, regular outreach to your community. I hope you also find it beneficial. You'll notice that I frequently refer to your "team." Don't be thrown by this. These are simply the people with whom you co-labor in the Gospel. Maybe they are part of your local church or members of a specific mission or local outreach team. Whatever the case, I'm betting that you don't do ministry all alone. I really hope not.

Now all that is left is to welcome you into this journey with me, and to thank you for taking the time. I am honored that you are reading - or even considering reading - this book. May Jesus be glorified in our lives more and more as we come to know Him better and more faithfully make Him known.

Tim Way
Tulsa, Oklahoma

From prayers that ask that I may be

Sheltered from the winds that beat on thee,

From fearing when I should aspire,

From faltering when I should climb higher,

From silken self, O Captain, free

Thy soldier who would follow thee.

From subtle love of softening things,

From easy choices, weakenings,

(Not thus are spirits fortified,

Not this way went the Crucified,)

From all that dims Thy Calvary,

Lamb of God, deliver me.

Give me the love that leads the way,

The faith that nothing can dismay

The hope no disappointments tire

The passion that will burn like fire,

Let me not sink to be a clod:

Make me Thy fuel, Flame of God[1]

By Amy Carmichael

---

[1] Amy Carmichael, quoted in *Celtic daily Prayer* (New York: Harper One, 2002), p 686.

1 THE FATHER

I stood there on the sidelines, in rapt attention. The African sun beat down, causing sweat to mingle with the tears that rolled down my cheeks. A few minutes earlier, my son -- then eight years old -- had taken the field in his very first "real" soccer game. A team of high school students from America had come to Uganda where we lived, to share about Christ -- and to play soccer. On this day my son was invited to join them as they took on the local village team. When called on he had proudly tossed his shoes aside before scampering onto the field. I was absolutely mesmerized as I stood there watching him. The overwhelming affection I have for him came pouring out through those tears. "What the heck!" I thought, "It's just a soccer game, for crying out loud." But that was my boy out there! I was so proud of him. I felt his every disappointment and every thrill during the next thirty minutes or so as powerfully as he did himself. I love him!

And yes, God loves me like that. He loves you like that. He loves it that you've signed up for this missions thing, or that you're participating in this local outreach. He feels your apprehension. He experiences your excitement. He will intimately know every disappointment and thrill, every fear and every temptation, every sacrifice and every victory. You affect Him. His heart is touched by you.

And not just with this whole missions deal. But when you go to work. When you step out to be friendly to a neighbor. When you fall in love and when you go on vacation. And when you screw up and get it all wrong He loves you. He loves you.

Jesus taught us to refer to God as a Father. I have five children. I cannot even begin to tell you how I love them. Words are pathetically insufficient. I cannot tell you how beautiful they are to me, or how much I love it when they sit on my lap or create a piece of art for me. I love them so much. I do not love them because they do a lot of stuff for me. As they grow older, they actually do become helpful around the house and in many other ways. But even so, their work does not come close to justifying the love I have for them. I simply love them and always have and always will. When they were younger, they really did not do any practical thing for me – but they did cause lots of problems and make lots of messes. And how I loved them! They were (and are) so adorable. I remember little things, like my four-year old walking into the room with his big mischievous smile and saying to me, "Daddy! Hey dude!" Melted my heart. I *love* that guy! These are my kids. I'd do anything for them. They have an effect on my heart that nobody else does.

One day when I came back home in the evening, my little son ran up to me, full of excitement. "Daddy, I know what your favorite color is!"

"Really? What is it?"

And he, full of confident excitement, responded, "It's GREEN!"

"You are so right! How did you know?" (I don't think I knew this fun fact about myself before that moment).

"And I know what your favorite animal is too!" Even more at a loss, I again inquired into this detail about myself of which I was apparently ignorant.

He enlightened me, "A rhinoceros!"

I affirmed.

And then came the kicker. With a look of pure delight and confidence, mixed with just the right touch of mischief and hope, he made it to the finale, "And I know who your favorite person is!"

At this point I was all smiles, but still a little unsure where this might go. As he squealed his answer, "ME!", he dove into my arms with a big smile on his face, and wrapped his little arms around my neck.

"You are absolutely right, Son. You are my favorite!"

And he is. My other kids are also my favorites, but that admission makes him no less so.

You are God's favorite.

We know that the greatest commandment is to love God. And yet there is something even more foundational. Something that must come first. We need to be confident of His love for us. The Bible says that it is experiencing and knowing His love for us that causes us to love. *"We love because God first loved us."* (1 John 4:19, NCV). It is His love that inspires and enables us to love.

"What marvelous love the Father has extended to us! Just look at it—we're called children of God! That's who we really are. But that's also why the world doesn't recognize us or take us seriously, because it has no idea who he is or what he's up to. But friends, that's exactly who we are: children of God. And that's only the beginning. Who knows how we'll end up!" (1 John 4:1-2, MSG)

Think about how awesome His love is! How unexpected! How extravagant! Can you hear the *Wow!* in John's words? Be captivated by His love for you. Meditate on it, even now. It's beyond reason. The living God is pursuing you. He likes you.

God sometimes uses marriage and the love of a man for his special woman as a way of describing His love for us. Officiating weddings is one of my favorite things. Recently I had that opportunity with a beautiful couple we have known for some time. As always, this wedding prodded me to think about the love of God. I came to realize afresh that I just do not get it.

God is seen as the passionate groom who faithfully loves and even lays down His life for His bride. There is something about that picture that does not easily register in my mind. But this is a significant part of God's self-revelation. He loves me. He loves me. He likes me. He wants me to be close to Him. To know me, and to be known by me. I must confess that this makes no sense whatsoever to me. Still, it is the truth, and is beyond way cool. It is hands down the best thing ever in the whole world.

The wedding thing gives me the impression that God pursues me. He woos me. He sacrifices for me. He wants good for me. He delights in me. He likes to hang out with me. I know, this feels ridiculous even to write such nonsense. But it's the Bible's view of God. And it's the view – or maybe a view – that He wants us to have. Because it is TRUE!

So, here's the thing: This seemingly ridiculous nonsense causes something in me – deep down inside – to light up at the thought. God likes me. God wants me. So who cares about the snub I received yesterday from someone whose opinion matters a lot to me? GOD thinks I'm cool. God is pursuing me. God loves me. I respond to this.

My friend Wendy responds to this too. Wendy is a tough lady in her forties, I think. She lives on the streets. She's had a rough life and is not sure how or where God might fit into it all. She has dealt with rejection and has been hurt a lot. For much of her life she's turned her back on God, and wanted nothing to do with Him. But now she is reaching out in hope – in the hope that maybe God loves her. That would make a world of difference, if God loved her. Maybe even enough of a difference for her to become a full-on, radical follower of Jesus. I am praying so.

In my life I often forget that Christianity is about God loving me. That's the root of it. Even before I get to my love for Him, it is God's love for me. That is what this thing is all about – that He loves me. Our faith often gets lost in services and songs and obligations and rules and doing right and serving and systems and principles and on and on. Those things are part of following Jesus. But there is so much more at the very heart of it all.

In a marriage, there are certainly principles and even rules to be followed. On Valentine's Day there's a "rule" that I give flowers or chocolate -- or preferably both -- to my wife. There's a rule that I tell her 'I love you' often. Another one that I spend time with her, and that we go out on dates. That we kiss before I leave the house in the morning, that I tell her she's beautiful, that we make love, that I don't call her fat when she's pregnant. But my marriage is so not about these rules. In fact, I obey them without even thinking of them as rules at all, or principles, or guidelines, or anything else. I do these things because I want to, because I love her and I want to please her and I love making her happy. Our marriage is all about love. And this love makes the giving of flowers or the washing of dishes or the earning of money full of meaning and value.

And following Jesus is like that. It really, really is. I do lots of stuff, and follow lots of principles... praying, giving, Bible-ing, and so on. Not doing things He hates. Trying to do stuff He loves – helping my neighbor, giving a meal to a homeless man, worshiping,... But it is so not about all that. It is about love – that He loves me. That He wants good for my life. That He gave His life for me, and He wants to be with me.

Whatever I do as a good Christian that is not done out of love for God is worthless. Totally worthless. And whatever supposedly 'secular' thing I do out of love for God has so much value. I can earn a paycheck or scrub a toilet or change a diaper or mow the grass or make a latte out of love for God. And it is so cool. I can do it giving thanks that He loves me.

You are God's favorite.

He loves you. Believe it! Trust it! *"We know how much God loves us, and we have put our trust in his love."* (1 Jn 4:16 NLT). You can experience His love, and you can trust it. You truly can! And when you do, you will begin to truly love God.

2 BEAUTIFUL WASTE

God's love is our identity. The most basic thing about who I am is that I am a child of God. I am loved by God. I am chosen by God. Jesus says, "*You did not choose me, but I chose you...*" (John 15:16a). I am desired by God. God believes in me. We sometimes talk of being sold-out for God, but what is more basic and more exhilarating is that God is sold-out for me! He has given His all for me. Jesus is "on fire" for you. That's why I love Him. How can I not respond to such amazing love? I am compelled to love Him back with my whole heart and mind and soul and strength. What does it mean to love God? How do I express this love to Him? Here are a few ideas:

First, I express my love to God through **worship**. I pour out my heart and life – abandoning myself to Him. I "waste" myself and all I have and all I am on Him. On one of the final evenings before His death, Jesus was relaxing in the home of a friend. A woman came to the table where He was, and poured out a jar of very expensive perfume onto His head.

"*When the disciples saw this, they were indignant. 'Why this waste?' they asked*" (Matt 26:8). I'd tend to agree with them. Especially when they added, "*This perfume could have been sold at a high price and the money given to the poor*" (v 9). Ouch. Who can argue with that?

This woman was clearly being foolish. But Jesus took her side! Jesus – the one who always defends the poor, who calls

7

His followers to love and care for them, whose heart is filled with compassion – Jesus took the woman's side. *"She has done a beautiful thing to me"* (v 10). True worship can appear foolish. I am not talking about the silly grin you have on your face while you sing to Him, but about what this worship can lead you to do with your life. It comes out of a heart of pure love and devotion. When I truly worship God, I see Him as everything to me. He is worth all that I have and so much more. He is worth all my time, my money, my possessions, my relationships, my dreams, my strength, my all. He's worth my life.

In the Old Testament, worship was primarily associated with sacrifice – the sacrifice of animals. In the New Testament worship is also primarily about sacrifice, but of a different kind. I myself am the sacrifice of worship.

"Therefore, I urge you, brothers and sisters, in view of God's mercy, to offer your bodies as a living sacrifice, holy and pleasing to God – this is your true and proper worship." (Rom 12:1). This is worship, and nothing less than this truly is. Offering myself as a living sacrifice means putting myself on the altar of death and giving up my life completely to God, so that He might fill me with His life. When I worship, I tell the Lord I am His, in every big and every little way. I love how The Message puts that verse:

"So here's what I want you to do, God helping you: Take your everyday, ordinary life—your sleeping, eating, going-to-work, and walking-around life—and place it before God as an offering."

Later in his life, Paul said, *"For I am already being poured out like a drink offering..."* (2 Tim 4:6). How I want to pour out my life for Him as an acceptable offering! We fill our lives with so many things, and we allow them to distract us from the main thing. In worship we express our love to God as a beautiful waste. I long for this to be true in the deepest parts of me.

Secondly, we express our love for God by *loving others*. Soak in these verses from the book of 1 John:

"We know that we have passed from death to life, because we love each other. Anyone who does not love remains in death... And this is how we know what love is: Jesus Christ laid down his life for us. And we ought to lay down our lives for our brothers and sisters." (3:14, 16)

"My dear, dear friends, if God loved us like this, we certainly ought to love each other. No one has seen God, ever. But if we love one another, God dwells deeply within us, and his love becomes complete in us—perfect love!" (4:11-12 – MSG)

"If anyone boasts, 'I love God,' and goes right on hating his brother or sister, thinking nothing of it, he is a liar. If he won't love the person he can see, how can he love the God he can't see? The command we have from Christ is blunt: Loving God includes loving people. You've got to love both." (4:20-21 – MSG).

The reality of our love for God is far beyond feeling or emotion. In actuality, we love God no more than we love the brother we love the least. *"Loving God includes loving people."* In Matthew 25, Jesus gives a picture of what is an exciting, but in some ways a disturbing, scene. He says that there will come a day when all peoples are gathered before Him, and He will separate them into two groups. He will praise one group and welcome them into Heaven, telling them that they helped Him when He was hungry, thirsty, homeless, naked, sick, and in prison. The other group will be condemned because they refused Him help. Apparently, none of the people in either group will have any memory of ever encountering Jesus in such need. His explanation is absolutely breathtaking:

"I'm telling the solemn truth: Whenever you did one of these things to someone overlooked or ignored, that was me—you did it to me." (Mat 25:40 - MSG). And to the other group, *"I'm telling the solemn truth: Whenever you failed to do one of these things to someone who was being overlooked or ignored, that was me—you failed to do it to me"* (v 45). Jesus is there – in His brothers and sisters who are in need. If we want to love God, we must express that love by loving people.

Thirdly, I love God through **obedience**.

"And we can be sure that we know him if we obey his commandments. If someone claims, "I know God," but doesn't obey God's commandments, that person is a liar and is not living in the truth. But those who obey God's word truly show how completely they love him. That is how we know we are living in him. Those who say they live in God should live their lives as Jesus did." (1 John 2:3-6 – NLT)

"Loving God means keeping his commandments, and his commandments are not burdensome." (1 John 5:3 – NLT)

"If you love me, obey my commandments... Those who accept my commandments and obey them are the ones who love me. And because they love me, my Father will love them. And I will love them and reveal myself to each of them." (John 14:15, 21 -- NLT)

This is kind of tough for us to take sometimes, but the Bible is very clear that we show our love for God by doing what He commands us. Righteousness is a result of His love for us, and in turn ours for Him. He does not love us because we are right, but we get right and live right because we love Him. All my service to Him comes out of a heart of love for Him. All my teaching and preaching and going and counseling, praying, working, helping, giving.

Fourthly, my love to God is expressed in a life of *holiness*. This is very much like the above, but deserves special attention. I become different because I love Him. I cannot truly change myself – I need Him. But I do open myself up for Him to change me, and I do this out of love for Him. Not because it will make my life better. I am not the center of this whole thing. Holiness is not about me. It is for Him and by Him.

Christianity is more about our hearts than anything else. Jesus said the greatest commandment is to love. God cares about our hearts. That leads to everything else, but the key thing is the heart. Where is the passion of the heart directed? What moves us, motivates us, makes us tick? Do we love Him? He is looking for people who simply and passionately love Him. Pure, holy, focused, love. Not distracted. It really is like a man and his bride. His primary desire is for her love – and for him to be her sole lover. No room for another. It is also like a Father with his kids. Yes, he wants obedience from them – but motivated by love. God wants our love. That is what we can give Him. For Him to be the central, sole, passionate, committed, faithful love of our hearts.

11

3 THE ROOT COMMAND

"Love must be sincere. Hate what is evil; cling to what is good. Be devoted to one another in brotherly love. Honor one another above yourselves." (Romans 12:9-10).

"If I could speak all the languages of earth and of angels, but didn't love others, I would only be a noisy gong or a clanging cymbal. If I had the gift of prophecy, and if I understood all of God's secret plans and possessed all knowledge, and if I had such faith that I could move mountains, but didn't love others, I would be nothing. If I gave everything I have to the poor and even sacrificed my body, I could boast about it; but if I didn't love others, I would have gained nothing.

"Love is patient and kind. Love is not jealous or boastful or proud or rude. It does not demand its own way. It is not irritable, and it keeps no record of being wronged. It does not rejoice about injustice but rejoices whenever the truth wins out. Love never gives up, never loses faith, is always hopeful, and endures through every circumstance.

"Prophecy and speaking in unknown languages and special knowledge will become useless. But love will last forever!" (1 Cor 13:1-8, NLT)

"We know what real love is because Jesus gave up his life for us. So we also ought to give up our lives for our brothers and sisters." 1 John 3:16 (NLT)

If you skimmed over those passages because they're so familiar – go back and try again. Soak it in. If you haven't figured it out, Jesus really wants you to love the rest of us. It'll be easy for a time. You may start to think your missions or ministry team or church is the awesomest ever. "Everyone just really loves Jesus and is so real and kind and FUN! These people are amazing!" Hey, they're probably even thinking the same thing about you. (That in itself should be a reality check).

The fact is, things change. And sometimes quickly. Eventually, there will be a struggle to love someone on your team. You may well be tempted to think it is not so important. On a big team, you can probably avoid them for the most part. Or, you may decide, "It's just a few more days until this is over, I'll just grit my teeth and bear it." But please remember this: *It is more important than you think.* There's more at work here than you just not getting along with someone.

John 13-17 gives us an amazing view into Jesus' last hours with His closest followers before He was crucified. He used this time to prepare them for the agonizing trial of the coming days, and to get them ready for the mission He was giving them in the world. Listen to a few of His comments on that fateful night:

"A new command I give you: Love one another. As I have loved you, so you must love one another. By this everyone will know that you are my disciples, if you love one another." John 13:34-35

"I've told you these things for a purpose: that my joy might be your joy, and your joy wholly mature. This is my command: Love one another the way I loved you. This is the very best way to love. Put your life on the line for your friends." John 15:11-13 (MSG).

"But remember the root command: Love one another." John 15:17 (MSG).

It was exceedingly important for them to get this message. Without loving one another, they would not accomplish what God intended in them and through them. In fact, the people of the world would not even really be able to know that these men were followers of Jesus without it. Years later, as we saw above, the apostle Paul wrote that without love we are nothing. The great "ministry" you do out there somewhere doesn't matter if you cannot love your team. You have accomplished nothing of eternal value. You can play with the orphans all you want, but without love for your brothers and sisters, you will lack the power to make a difference. You can preach or hammer or doctor your heart out, but without love it's just not going to count. The people might think well of you. They might honor you and appreciate you. You might get a good feeling about what you have done. But there will be no eternal value.

Your ability to minister in genuine spiritual power is more linked to the strength of your love than the greatness of your gifts. In fact, it's better for you to accomplish nothing visibly while in the country, but to walk in love, than to finish some giant task without love. Let it be your focus. Make this your battle cry: Love God. Love my team. Love the people.

There is an enemy who is tenaciously fighting against your team unity. He will try to bring strife, jealousy, competition, offense, and anything else in order to disrupt what God is doing. One of the very best ways he has of keeping you from being fruitful is to bring un-love into your team. He will be a determined foe, and will doggedly continue to harass until he has worn you down. You must also therefore be diligent and resolute in your defenses. Fight for harmony and peace and loving one another. Here are a few thoughts to help your team operate in God's love as you serve side by side with your very human brothers and sisters:

1   *Loving your team is not dependent on your team.* Not one bit. Your love for them has nothing to do with whether or not they deserve it. They will probably deserve it sometimes and not other times. It is irrelevant. Their loveliness is not what gives you the ability to love them truly. It is God's love in you. He loves them all – including you – all the time. When we are great and when we are really, really not. "God demonstrates his own love for us in this: While we were still sinners, Christ died for us." (Rom 5:8). And remember this, the Bible tells us that just as Jesus gave up his life for us, we are to do so for our brothers! (1 John 3:16). His love is unconditional and it is always.

2   *Submit to authority.* I know. Believe me, I know. This one can be a sore trial. I dare not even relate my failures in this area. But it really does affect the mission. You can disagree with your leaders, and you can discuss, but at the end of the day just smile and follow. Even if he is being a complete idiot.

Obey your leaders and submit to them, for they keep watch over your souls as those who will give an account. Let them do this with joy and not with grief, for this would be unprofitable for you. (Hebrews 13:17 - NASB).

Have you ever had a leader who loved scriptures like this just a little too much? Well, even then, it truly is vitally important that you heed it in all humility. Doing so will increase your team's effectiveness. Failing in this area will greatly hinder your work.

3   *Be authentic and full of grace.* Being on a missions trip or part of a local outreach, we all want to put our best spiritual foot forward, and that's a good thing. But at the same time, none of us are spiritual giants (Well, there may be one or two on your team, but not most of us). Let's create an atmosphere of openness. Of acceptance. Helping and exhorting, but not condemning. Challenging, but not nagging. Let's be broken before one another. Tear off the masks and be ourselves.

People are going to disappoint you even if you are only together for a short time. Expect it. You will be tempted to get hurt or offended or annoyed. Instead, choose grace. Remember that we all need Jesus just to stay saved, let alone be a fruitful missionary. Be quick to forgive and quick to repent. Even if you feel you are only 1% responsible for a conflict, and the other person is 99% responsible, repent of your part. Then, in humility and love, tell your perspective and how the other person made you feel when he said what he did. Do not allow small wounds to fester. No matter how the other receives this, determine to show him respect and love. If a problem persists, speak to one of your leaders and enlist their help.

4 **Walk in humility** toward one another. *"Be humble, thinking of others as better than yourselves."* (Phil 2:3b - NLT). That about says it all. Think about it. Read it again. What if we all actually did that?

5 **Pray like a madman.** Pray for the other members of your team – especially the ones you have the hardest time with. Also pray for God's love to so fill you that you find Him loving others through you. Get desperate for this. One wise father gave this advice to his son:

> "Son, never deal with problems of disunity until you pray people's hearts ready to receive correction. God will do most of the work of unity if you do the work of prayer."[2]

Several years ago, I was leading a local outreach team that partnered with a successful businessman to minister in an impoverished part of town. By the time we were just a few months into this partnership, the man and his friends had become exasperated with my team of young men -- and not without reason. We were immature and lacked initiative, tended to sullenness, and were short on diligence. To be fair, I knew our guys were growing and maturing in Christ, but it was sometimes painfully slow.

This man lost all patience with us. He would become angry, nitpick every little thing, and cut my guys with bitter words. He and I had multiple confrontations. I came to dread

---

[2] Floyd McClung, *Leading Like Jesus* (Follow Publications, Kindle version, 2015), Location 2081.

every encounter, and our team was filled with discouragement and ready to quit. Instead, we determined to pray for this man and the situation. We prayed regularly. We prayed together and we prayed individually. One day we were called in to yet another meeting, and we gathered with apprehension once again, waiting to be regaled with all of our recent failures. But that is not what happened this time. In one of the greatest demonstrations of humility I have ever seen, this older, successful, wealthy, powerful man repented to a group of young ragamuffins. Tears flowed. Apologies began to fly both ways. And from that day on, we worked in mutual respect and love. We really did. I am convinced that the keys were determined prayer and broken hearts.

4 FRUITFUL MINISTRY

"You did not choose me, but I chose you and appointed you to go and bear fruit – fruit that will last. Then the Father will give you whatever you ask in my name." – John 15:16

Holy schmoly! This is very cool. Jesus chose you and He appointed you to bear fruit that will last. You. This is His dream for you. And by the way, just ask the Father for what you need, and He will give it to you. And I love what He said a minute before (verse 8): "This is to my Father's glory, that you bear much fruit, showing yourselves to be my disciples." God gets glory when you bear fruit. I'm telling you the truth: I want Jesus to get glory through my life. I really want it. More than anything. I live for His glory. If you back up even further in John 15, you will find that the thing that will cause you to bear fruit is abiding in Jesus. Just hanging with Him all the time. Putting your attention onto Him. Thinking about Him. Talking to Him. Listening to Him. Obeying Him. Looking for Him. Submitting to Him. Remaining in Him when everything around you is swirling. Doing everything for Him and with Him and in Him. It is so great. Abide in Jesus and you bear fruit. Bear fruit and you glorify God. The secret to life. You were *chosen* for this. *Appointed* for it. Sweet.

Practice this and you cannot go wrong. The acknowledged presence of God in your life is the key to everything. Without that, all of your skills and abilities and resources and effort and sacrifices will be worthless. You can follow all the right ministry principles and serve with cultural sensitivity, but without Him it will not be fruitful. *"Apart from me you can do nothing"* (John 15:5b). That's pretty blunt. But with Him, everything changes. Everything is permeated with power. With life. Seek after it. Set your heart on abiding in Jesus. Do not allow distractions or fatigue or conflict or trouble or ease or anything keep you from seeking to live in the knowledge of His presence continually.

Years ago, my family and I lived in Uganda. And I hated doing dishes. At one point, I was challenged by the simple idea of doing everything -- *everything* -- for the glory of God, and out of love for Him. Eventually it dawned on me that doing dishes was part of everything. On Sunday mornings, I would often preach in a local church in the city of Kampala. We would have breakfast together as a family, and I would inform my wife and kids that I had to "spiritually prepare" to minister, or some such nonsense, so I would not be able to help with the breakfast dishes. And then this revelation came: maybe the best "spiritual preparation" I could do would be to do the dishes for my family, *out of love for Jesus.* I soon became convinced that this simple discipline did more for my heart than anything else I could have tried on those hectic mornings. I was learning to acknowledge that the posture of my heart towards Jesus is the one thing that makes any activity holy or spiritual. If I could not do the dishes out of love for Jesus, neither could I preach His Word out of love for Him, or with any measure of power to bear fruit.

Now, we know that God is always with us. So what does it mean to desire His presence? To abide in Him? It means, at least in part, to acknowledge Him. To pay attention to Him. To understand that, although He never leaves us, there are many times when He is not exactly obvious. Isaiah prayed, "Truly you are a God who hides himself, O God and Savior of Israel" (Isaiah 45:15). Have you ever felt so? Sometimes this is about the most relatable scripture in the whole Bible for me. God, why would you hide from me?

I do not always feel the presence of God, and my guess is that neither do you. There are times when I do, and it is wonderful. Maybe it happens during corporate worship, or in a time of private intercession. On occasion I've been surprised by it in the midst of a group Bible study with the homeless, or as part of a simple prayer for a person in need. But these instances are anything but constant. Most of the hours in most of my days are... normal. Mundane. Not spiritual. I feel things, sure. I feel tired or I feel frustrated or happy or excited or angry or confused or alone. But it is all very, very *natural*. Typical. And yet... And yet.

Again, I have to ask, why do I not experience Him all the time, or at least a lot of the time? Why must my *feelings* suggest that He is more distant than near, more transcendent than immanent? Why might the "Savior of Israel" hide from His people?

So that they would seek Him.

"You will seek me and find me when you seek me with all your heart." -- Jeremiah 29:13

"From one man he made all the nations, that they should inhabit the whole earth; and he marked out

21

their appointed times in history and the boundaries of their lands. God did this so that they would seek him and perhaps reach out for him and find him, though he is not far from any one of us." -- Acts 17:26-27

God wants you to move towards Him. Yes, he pursues you. He has already done all that is necessary for your salvation and acceptance. His Spirit is active to convict and invite. And because of this, we need to make an effort. We need to train ourselves to notice the Father, to develop the discipline of acknowledging the presence of Jesus, to build the habit of carrying on a conversation with the Holy Spirit.

He is present. This is one of the great revelations of God throughout the scriptures. He is present! His desire has always been to dwell in the midst of His people -- from Eden to the wilderness tabernacle to the temple in Jerusalem to the very incarnation itself to the pouring out of the Spirit and the establishment of the Church, God is screaming His desire and His dogged determination to be with us. Though He hides, He will be found. It reminds me of playing hide and seek with my children when they were small. The joy for me, as a father, was not in finding a place they could never discover. The joy was in being found, and I would manipulate the game to that end. Today, you are invited by the Creator of the universe into a cosmic, rigged game of hide-and-seek. But it is more than a game. In fact, everything rides on your participation.

Jesus is the answer to your deepest longings. He is the provision for your most desperate needs. He is the peace in the face of your most profound fears. Jesus is more than you can possibly imagine. He is more powerful and more holy. More beautiful and more majestic. He is more merciful and He is more loving. And He is this towards you. Look to Him today. When you are frustrated in your attempts to be good or to do right, He is sufficient. When you are confused about circumstances or simply do not know what to do, His presence really is enough. When you are hurt or broken or discouraged, He is your healer and your life. Look to Him! You do not need all the answers, and you do not need to figure out all the whys and why nots. You need Jesus. You need to train your mind to look to Him. Abide in Him. Remember, the greatest truth is that He loves you.

Take time this week to truly study John 15, and trust the Lord to speak to you through it.

"For many years I was bothered by the thought that I was a failure at prayer. Then one day I realized I would always be a failure at prayer and I've gotten along much better ever since."
-- Brother Lawrence[3]

"I have posted watchmen on your walls, O Jerusalem; they will never be silent day or night. You who call on the Lord, give yourselves no rest, and give him no rest till he establishes Jerusalem and makes her the praise of the earth."
-- Isaiah 62:6-7

"The rest which flows from unceasing prayer, needs to be sought at all costs, even when the flesh is itchy, the world is alluring and the demons noisy."
-- Henry Nouwen[4]

[3] Brother Lawrence, *The Practice of the Presence of God* (New Kensington, PA: Whitaker House, 1982).
[4] Henry J.M. Nouwen, *The Way of the Heart* (London: Longman and Todd, 1999), p 60.

5 INTERCESSION

As discussed in the last section, a lifestyle of personal prayer and abiding in Jesus are essential to your mission. A day-by-day and moment-by-moment relationship with Jesus is the center out of which all else flows. However, there is even more to it. You need to zealously intercede for others in a disciplined and committed way, and you need to recruit others to pray for you and your mission.

First, you must learn the habit of intercession. It may be difficult to maintain at first, but persevere. It is so worth it. Pray for the Lord to transform hearts, to change circumstances, to draw people to Himself, to work miracles for His glory. Pray for His kingdom -- His rule -- to come into the lives of people. Pray for them by name when you can. Pray in faith. Andrew Murray wrote this:

> "There is a twofold use of prayer: the one, to obtain strength and blessing for our own life; the other, the higher, the true glory of prayer, for which Christ has taken us into His fellowship and teaching, is intercession, where prayer is the royal power a child of God exercises in heaven on behalf of others and even of the kingdom."[5]

---

[5] Andrew Murray, *With Christ in the School of Prayer* (Redford, VA: Wilder Publications, 2008), p 37.

Intercession is powerful for several reasons. Consider the following:

Intercession joins you to the work of Jesus.

"Who then is the one who condemns? No one. Christ Jesus who died—more than that, who was raised to life— is at the right hand of God and is also interceding for us." (Romans 8:34).

Jesus is interceding, and you can join Him in this great work!

Intercession changes us. As you pray for others, your heart becomes more open to the work of the Spirit in your own life. You receive His compassion and love and mercy towards others; even His sadness and His yearning for people. Your heart becomes filled with His desires and passions and you are more able to deny yourself and your own self-centered impulses. The heart of the Father is for people and He wants to share that heart with you. What a privilege!

I love to walk the streets of my city and pray for the people who live and work here. Every Thursday evening my friends and I host a meal for the poor and the homeless, and we sit and eat together. I have been doing this now for more than eight years, and have developed friendships with many people who live on the streets. And yet, in spite of my experience and all the powerful and tender moments I have shared with them, my heart still leans towards fear and judgment when I encounter a homeless person. I feel ashamed and embarrassed to confess this, but it is the truth. I hate it, and yet cannot control it by an act of my will. And so I pray for the poor as I walk, and it is in this intercession that my heart moves from fear to compassion, from judgment to grace, from pride to humility. It is only as I pray for them that the transformation occurs. You have to intercede for others, because through it God will make you someone He can use.

Intercession changes them. This is perhaps the most mysterious part of ministry to me. I do not understand it, and I do not know how it happens. Yet I am convinced that the Father responds to my desperate prayers on behalf of others, and He intervenes. He protects them from harm. He provides what they need. And -- here is the mystery -- He transforms their hearts. Someone who is resistant to Jesus becomes open. Someone who is ambivalent becomes desperate. Someone locked in pride becomes repentant. It happens. There is usually more happening than prayer -- the Gospel is being proclaimed and the compassion and mercy of Jesus are being demonstrated. But intercession is an essential element, and other activities tend to lack power without it.

In my role as disciple-maker, I sometimes have had to confront someone over an issue of sinful behavior or wrong thinking or unloving attitudes. I hate this, and honestly am not good at it. I approach such meetings with fear and trembling, my heart filling with dread as I introduce the discussion. And yet, I have found an amazing and wonderful secret that has often infused these unwanted conversations with power and grace. Intercession.

When I become aware of an issue in someone's life -- particularly a person that I am shepherding, I am learning that my first step is to pray. As I pray for the person, as mentioned above, multiple things happen. For real. I have seen this pattern many times. First, I join with Jesus in His work on behalf of the person. Then, my heart turns from anger or hurt or disappointment, back to love and grace and understanding.

This in itself is huge. My love for the person is renewed. As I continue praying over a period of several days or more, sometimes I become convinced that there is no other step for me to take -- the only thing I am called to do is pray. At other times, I become more convinced that a conversation is necessary. And here is where the mystery is for me -- I have come to these encounters, bathed in prayer, to find the person's heart soft and completely prepared. Sometimes all I have had to do is utter one sentence, and the other person has begun to repent. Other times it takes more, but the end result is often the same. God works in mysterious ways as we pray for the hearts of people.

In addition to practicing intercession for those you intend to reach, you must -- you *must* -- gather a team of faithful people to pray for you.
"A prayer movement precedes every disciple-making movement."[6]

"If you are a disciple-maker, you need to recruit, train, and mobilize an extensive prayer network—whether you earn your living as a disciple-maker or earn it another way. If you do not have a well-developed prayer network, you will be frustrated and disappointed as a disciple-maker."[7]

Paul seems to have been convinced that this was true. He often urged the churches to pray for him and the mission to which he was giving his life:
"Pray also for me, that whenever I speak, words may be given me so that I will fearlessly make known the mystery

---

[6] David Watson and Paul Watson, *Contagious Disciple-Making* (Nashville: Thomas Nelson, 2014), pg 79.
[7] ibid, 90.

of the gospel, for which I am an ambassador in chains. Pray that I may declare it fearlessly, as I should." -- Ephesians 6:19-20

"And pray for us, too, that God may open a door for our message, so that we may proclaim the mystery of Christ, for which I am in chains. Pray that I may proclaim it clearly, as I should." -- Colossians 4:3-4

"Brothers and sisters, pray for us." -- 1 Thessalonians 5:25

"As for other matters, brothers and sisters, pray for us that the message of the Lord may spread rapidly and be honored, just as it was with you. And pray that we may be delivered from wicked and evil people, for not everyone has faith." -- 2 Thessalonians 3:1-2

Who do you know that will partner with you in intercession for the mission you are on? Who will faithfully pray for 'God to open a door for [your] message,' for you to 'fearlessly make known the mystery of the gospel?' Take a few minutes to ask the Father to bring such people to your mind. Then brainstorm a list, and pray over it. Begin to contact these people, explain to them what you are doing, and invite them into partnership with you. Be committed to sending this critical group regular updates, specific prayer requests, and reports of answered prayer. A simple group text can make a significant difference.

If you truly want the power of God to be evident in your outreach, and lasting fruit from your efforts, you must give ample attention to prayer and intercession.

6 WHAT'S SO GREAT ABOUT THE GOSPEL?

I was sitting in a church service as the pastor gave a passionate invitation for people to come and give their lives to Jesus. The worship band was playing appropriate 'come to the altar music' in the background. Two teenagers were involved in a lively discussion of their own in the row in front of me. Well, not really a discussion. One of them was doing everything he could to get his companion to go to the front with him and 'get saved.' The other was stubbornly quiet. The 'evangelist' teen was soon reduced to pleading. "Oh come to the front! Why won't you come to the front and get saved?" And then in apparent desperation he let it all out in one fantastic promise: "If you come to the front and get saved, God will give you whatever you want! Why would you not want that?" His friend remained unmoved.

As I sat listening to this conversation, I was trapped between two emotions. The first was that I loved the zeal of this young evangelist. I was challenged by it. I loved his enthusiasm, his desperate desire to see his friend come to Jesus. It was beautiful. I found myself longing for the same kind of boldness and passion in my own feeble attempts at sharing the Gospel. But there was also an incredible sadness. This is what the Gospel is reduced to? "Come to the front and get saved and God will give you whatever you want?" Really?

29

Is that the best we can do? Do we followers of Jesus even know the Gospel we have been commissioned to proclaim?

What is this news that is so great we would spend thousands of dollars and travel half-way around the world to tell it to people we have never even met? What is it that would cause multitudes of people over the course of history to lose their lives because of their insistence on shouting this message? What is this Gospel? Paul said that he was not ashamed of it, because it is the power of God to salvation (Rom 1:16). There is one current movement of Chinese missionaries who are so determined to make it known that "They are not only willing to die for the gospel, they are expecting it."[8] The Gospel is powerful!

Yes, the Gospel is powerful. And yet, to many, it has become blasé. Barely relevant. Boring. Listen to Shane Claiborne:

> "God forgive us for all those we have lost because we made the Gospel boring. I am convinced that if we lose kids to the culture of drugs and materialism, of violence and war, it's because we don't dare them, not because we don't entertain them. It's because we make the Gospel too easy, not because we make it too difficult."[9]

The Gospel is of immeasurable value. We must strive to handle it well. To present it rightly. The Gospel has the power to transform lives, to change communities and nations, and to lead us to eternal life. So what is it?

---

[8] David Livermore, *Serving with Eyes Wide Open* (Grand Rapids: Baker Books, 2006), p 53.
[9] Shane Claiborne, *The Irresistible Revolution* (Grand Rapids: Zondervan, 2006), pg 224.

The Gospel is first of all a story, and it is vital that we know it, inside and out. We will look at that more in the next chapter. It is our story, and it

> "is going out all over the world. It is bearing fruit everywhere by changing lives, just as it changed your lives from the day you first heard and understood the truth about God's wonderful grace." (Colossians 1:6 NLT).

All the ministry that we do must be seen within the framework of this riveting, transforming story.

In its simplest form, the Gospel is simply that God loves you and is inviting you into His family – that He would adopt you as His own special child. The invitation is to enter into a relationship with God through Jesus Christ. The reality is that you can know God and be known by Him. Think about that. To know God. To know what He is like and to experience Him. He is willing and deeply desiring to reveal Himself to you. To know God is to experience the power that created the universe and raised Jesus from the dead. It is to be forgiven of all sin and to be free from accusation. It is to walk with the King. It is to know love and peace and joy beyond description. And to be known by Him. Known and accepted. It is to experience love with no strings attached. For God knows everything about you, and yet He loves you more than anyone has ever loved you. To be known by God is to be clean, to be free from all residue of guilt and shame. The Gospel is that you are wanted. Wanted by God Himself. You are loved by the most beautiful and awe-inspiring and powerful being there is. The Gospel is an invitation. It is summarized in the word "come." "Come and be with me," God says. And He says it to you.

"Therefore, if anyone is in Christ, the new creation has come: The old has gone, the new is here! All this is from God, who reconciled us to himself through Christ and gave us the ministry of reconciliation: that God was reconciling the world to himself in Christ, not counting people's sins against them. And he has committed to us the message of reconciliation. We are therefore Christ's ambassadors, as though God were making his appeal through us. We implore you on Christ's behalf: Be reconciled to God. God made him who had no sin to be sin for us, so that in him we might become the righteousness of God." -- 2 Cor 5:17-21

When we respond to this invitation to come to God, He does a lot of stuff. He makes us completely new. He gives us a fresh start on life with a clean slate, just as though we had never sinned. And by the way, that word keeps coming up: Sin. What does sin have to do with the Gospel? Well, if the Gospel is that God is reconciling us to Himself, there must be something that has been separating us. And that is sin. Sin is our failure to bow our knee to Him. It is our failure to love Him. It is not meeting His standards of behavior and virtue. It is our hatred and greed and lust and dishonesty and disrespect and selfishness. It is our pride. It is our thinking that we can get along without our Creator and our not trusting in the God who loves us. It is every unloving and ungodly thing we have ever done, said, or thought. And we are full of it.

This sin has a power in our lives. It is the power of death. It keeps us from the source of life, God Himself, and it leads us ultimately to eternal death and separation from God. It is hideous. And we are full of it.

But God has intervened. He has made a way out for all of us. It was not an easy rescue. It cost Him a lot. It required that Jesus live a perfect life with no sin and then die a horrendous death with all the sin of all humanity piled onto Him. He was covered with guilt and shame, though it was not His. He suffered and died on the cross, bearing the consequences of our misdeeds. But after three days He defeated death by rising again into life.

So the big problem of sin has been totally dealt with. God has done it! And thus comes the Gospel, the invitation. "Come!" God calls. Wow. What is left is for us to respond to it.

How do we come? First, by *believing* and trusting God. This is not mere vocal adherence to a creed or the repetition of a mantra, but a genuine decision to trust Him for salvation. It is trusting that this whole Gospel thing is all true, and that God really has torn down the dividing wall between the divine and the human. Believe that Jesus died for my sins and rose again and is alive now. Trust that there truly is nothing more to be done in regards to my sin, my failures, my weaknesses. Trust that God's ways are better. Trust that He will care for me and that He will give me eternal life and that He will be with me. Trust that I will be His child. Believe what He says!

Then we need to *repent*. That simply means to turn away from the stuff that God does not like. We turn from a false way of thinking and seeing the world, to the right way. We make a decision that from now on we are not going our way anymore, but God's way. We will mess up from time to time still. We will be hard pressed to live up to our commitment. But the key is that we have turned. We are moving in a different direction. We are choosing God because He chose us.

And finally, we need to *follow*. Coming to Jesus means submitting to Him – it means He is in charge. We cannot come any other way. No compromising with Him. No half-way. We realize that our life belongs to Him, and we determine that He will rule us. This sounds a little scary to some, but it takes us back to the first part – trusting Him. His rule will lead us into life. Our own rule – or in reality, the rule of our sinful nature – will only lead to death.

> "When you were slaves to sin, you were free from the obligation to do right. And what was the result? You are now ashamed of the things you used to do, things that end in eternal doom. But now you are free from the power of sin and have become slaves of God. Now you do those things that lead to holiness and result in eternal life. For the wages of sin is death, but the free gift of God is eternal life through Christ Jesus our Lord." -- Romans 6:20-23 (NLT).

God is looking for us to love Him with all our hearts. When we love Him, other things kind of come almost naturally. Our love for Him is what leads us to leave what He hates (repent) and to follow Him (submit). Saying 'yes' to Jesus' call to come is very much like a girl saying "yes" to the proposal of the one she loves. That "yes" will lead her into a lot of different things, but the bottom line of it all is love. She says yes to him because she loves him, and that love will lead her into all that follows.

The Gospel is God's invitation to every person on the planet, and the only appropriate response to it is to drop everything and run to accept it.

7 GOSPEL STORY

What is the Gospel? What do you do when called upon to share it? In the last section we discussed the invitational nature of the Gospel, and that is essential. We also need to know that the Gospel is a story. When we proclaim the Gospel, we are telling God's story. You can share how your life has been changed -- and that certainly is good news. But please remember that ultimately the Gospel is about Jesus. It is His story, and His promise. Share your story, but do not neglect His.

When we lived in Uganda, I would often participate in evangelistic outreaches with local churches. We did a lot of this when we hosted teams of short-term missionaries from the States. Typically, the scenario would be something like this: We would gather at the church and divide into different teams. Usually the team would consist of a couple of us Americans, a member or two of the local church, and someone to translate for the foreigners. We would then head out into the community. Approaching a hut or small shop, the church member would engage in conversation with whoever we met. At some point, he would turn to the Americans, and say, "Ok, they are ready."

"Ummm. Ready for what?"

"For you to share the Gospel. Go ahead."

The first few times I experienced this, I would awkwardly stumble around trying to think of something to say, feeling ridiculous. Eventually it dawned on me that I should probably figure out what the Gospel is, and simply share it. That turned out to be a good idea.

So, what is the Gospel that we have been commissioned to proclaim?

First Matter

God created Man in His own image, to know Him and enjoy fellowship with Him. He gave Man the task of stewarding His creation. Man sinned against God by disobeying His clear command. Because of this act of rebellion, evil and darkness were let loose in the world. Man's pure and intimate fellowship with God was broken, and from that time all people have been born with a propensity to sin. In fact, all people continued to rebel against God. All that is not right in the world can be traced back to this rebellion -- all the violence, injustice, wickedness, rejection, sickness, poverty, perversion, and depression -- in fact, all that brings misery and brokenness to mankind. Man's sin is the root cause. Creation has been spoiled, twisted to the point that its original intent, design, and beauty can be difficult to see.

God began the work of redemption by choosing one people to bless, that through them He might bless all nations. He chose Abraham and his descendants, who became the people of Israel. Through them God revealed Himself to humanity in new ways. He delivered Israel from slavery in Egypt. He gave them the Law. He dwelt among them in the Tabernacle, and later in the Temple. He provided a land for them, and formed them into a nation. They in turn continually rebelled against His rule, and failed to represent Him in the world. God sent prophets and other righteous ones to remind and warn them, but these were largely ignored. Eventually, God judged His people by removing them from their land and putting them in the hands of foreign oppressors. Then He sent His Son.

The Good News

God continued to love all people deeply. He sent His Son, Jesus Christ, to reveal His love and to rescue people from the destruction they had wrought. Jesus is God's very Son, and he became a man, born of a virgin. He lived a perfect life, obeying His divine Father in every detail. In doing so, He revealed to us exactly what the Father is like. He also showed us how we as people are meant to live, empowered by the Spirit of God. More than that, He lived perfectly for us. He lived perfectly so that He could give us His perfection in exchange for our sin. And that's what happened when He died.

He gave Himself to be killed on the cross, and in so doing He made an exchange with us. We are offered His righteousness -- His rightness -- and all the rewards that come with that. And He took our sin -- and the punishment that came with that. He took the blame for all the selfishness, pride, and rebellion that has ever been committed. He took our shame and guilt and condemnation and brokenness, and in exchange we received His purity and wholeness and rightness. There is no condemnation for us now. Not for the sin committed ten years ago, or the one committed a minute ago -- or even for the one that will be committed tomorrow. No condemnation. No guilt. No shame.

God Himself died and was buried in a tomb -- the darkest and most hopeless situation imaginable -- but He rose again.

He conquered sin and all that is most vile. Jesus rose bodily from the dead, forever defeating death and winning eternal life for all who would believe. We are people of resurrection, people of hope. Jesus ascended to Heaven. He is preparing a place for us and for all who believe. We have a home with Jesus. He is interceding for us to the Father, securing salvation for all who believe.

Jesus also sent His Spirit to dwell inside of us. The very same Spirit that raised Jesus from the dead lives within all who believe. Right now. And always. Because of this, we can live a life of victory over sin. A life filled with things like love and joy and peace and kindness and faithfulness. A life of power and of witnessing to the reality of Jesus. Together, filled with the Spirit of God, we can reveal to the world what He is truly like. That is our calling and our privilege and our duty and our destiny.

Jesus is coming again as judge and king. At that time, He will gather all who belong to Him to be with Him forever, while everyone else will be cast aside. He is going to make everything right. None of the evil in this world is going to survive. Injustice of every kind will be banished. No more poverty. Or sickness. Violence. Hatred. Pain. Depression. Fear. It is all overcome, and will be no more. Instead there will be joy and peace and goodness. There will be love and plenty and satisfaction. There will be true rest and true work and true relationship. True worship and true celebration. Those who have put their trust in Him will be with Him forever, and those who have rejected Him will be forever separated.

Response

In order to receive the amazing benefits of the Gospel, a person must believe, putting his complete trust in Jesus and what He has done. Faith in Jesus is the only way to be saved from the ravages of sin, which eventually result in eternal death. When a person decides to believe and submit to Christ, turning away from his old way of thinking and living, the Holy Spirit comes to dwell within him. The Spirit leads the person to live a life according to the pattern and teaching of Jesus as seen in the writings of the New Testament. He also empowers the believer to witness to the reality of Christ through proclaiming the Gospel. Those who choose to put their faith in Jesus demonstrate this in the act of being baptized.

8 WINNING THE LOST

For the Son of Man came to seek and to save what was lost – Lk 19:10

Jesus loves the lost. He loves people who don't know Him. He loves people who do not care about Him. People who do not believe in Him. People who hate Him. People who mock Him. He loves people on drugs. He loves gay people. He loves the promiscuous. He loves prostitutes, and even the ones who use and abuse them. He sees past what they do, deep down into who they are. He loves politicians. He loves politicians who fight for abortion rights and banning prayer in schools. He loves Hindus and Mormons and Muslims and atheists and agnostics and Buddhists and Baptists and Pentecostals and Methodists and Catholics. He loves terrorists. He loves terrorists who kill Americans. He loves the worst of us. He loves me.

You have a lot to give as you seek to minister to others, but nothing compares with the gift of the Gospel. Some of you may be performing dramas and preaching and witnessing one-on-one. Others may be caring for the sick, showing love to orphans, constructing a building, feeding the homeless, fixing people's hair, repairing computers, surfing, playing soccer, teaching English, or any of dozens of other acts of service. But in all things be conscious of the fact that God wants you to share the Gospel. He wants you to seek out the lost and to lead them to salvation in Jesus. He loves them, but He is separated from them. This separation will be eternal unless they repent (Matt 25:41-46; 2 Thess 1:9; Rev 20:15). He is calling you to be a messenger of reconciliation (see 2 Cor 5:16-21). How are you to do this? No matter what your particular area of service, here are some thoughts that can help you to win the lost for the glory of Jesus:

One: *Pray your guts out.* Evangelism is spiritual work and it requires spiritual power. The devil does not want you to go around rescuing people from his dominion, and he is laboring to prevent it.

"The god of this age has blinded the minds of unbelievers, so that they cannot see the light of the gospel of the glory of Christ, who is the image of God. For we do not preach ourselves, but Jesus Christ as Lord, and ourselves as your servants for Jesus' sake. For God, who said, 'Let light shine out of darkness,' made his light shine in our hearts to give us the light of the knowledge of the glory of God in the face of Christ." -- 2 Corinthians 4:4-6

We need to pray for God's power to remove the blinders from people's minds so that they can see the truth – so that they can see Jesus as He is. As we saw in a previous chapter, Paul the great apostle was always asking people to pray for him as he preached the Gospel:

"Pray also for me, that whenever I open my mouth, words may be given me so that I will fearlessly make known the mystery of the gospel..." Eph 6:19

"And pray for us, too, that God may open a door for our message, so that we may proclaim the mystery of Christ, for which I am in chains. Pray that I may proclaim it clearly, as I should." Col 4:3-4

"Finally, brothers, pray for us that the message of the Lord may spread rapidly and be honored, just as it was with you." 2 Thess 3:1

Prayer represents a tension between grace and striving. Paul tells the Colossians that Epaphras *"is always wrestling in prayer for you"* (Colossians 4:12). That sounds like work: Wrestling, effort, sweat. This was no quick bed-time prayer: "God bless the Colossians." This was hard labor. And yet, prayer is in itself an admission that we cannot do something – that we need help. It is an appeal to the grace of God. We have nothing to offer to induce Him to answer us. We are left to rely on God's grace, and in truth we are desperate for it. It is only His grace that can save a person. Work to bring God's grace to bear in the people you are out to serve. It is an odd thing -- to work at being powerless and needy -- but that is the position we are in. Our tendency is to self-sufficiency, yet we are profoundly not sufficient. Prayer may well be the most difficult part of your ministry, but it is the most important. Pray for the lost. Pray for the people you encounter. Pray for the people you see every day. Believe that God's Spirit is hearing you and is at work.

Two: *Introduce people to Jesus.* Make this all about Him – because it is. You are not there to simply share a plan or a principle, but to introduce a person. Jesus. Always get back to Him. Find ways to express and demonstrate His love. Let His goodness and love and power flow through you. Bring Him up in normal conversation just as you would with a Christian friend. He is the center of your life, and is involved in all of it. Do not hide this from people you are getting to know.

Three: *Share the Gospel.*
"For I am not ashamed of the gospel, because it is the power of God that brings salvation to everyone who believes: first to the Jew, then to the Gentile." -- Romans 1:16

In all of our serving and building relationships and demonstrating love, we have to get around to telling the story of Jesus. Sharing the Gospel is the path to salvation. It is, as we have seen, the invitation to believe and submit. It brings people to a point of decision. You can share the basics of the Gospel in just a few minutes or you can spend hours delving in more deeply. But we have to learn to speak the Gospel to people: to talk about the birth, life, death, burial, resurrection, ascension, and promised return of Jesus.

Four: *Care about the person.* And show it. Encourage two-way conversation. Find out about them. Be genuinely concerned. Do not give the impression that you're after them like a salesperson or a politician. This is not about you. It is about Jesus and it is about the person to whom you are speaking. Take time with people. Show compassion. Show interest. Listen. Let them teach you something. If on an international mission, speak to them in their native language as much as you can, even if it's just to say, "Hello." Maybe they can teach you some more of it. If you are ministering to the poor in your own city, listen to their stories. Seek to understand something about their life and their culture and world view. Be wowed by them. Look for signs of the image of God in them. Be fascinated.

Five: *Share your testimony.* Make it personal. Tell about what God has done in your life. Share from your heart. Think about this ahead of time. Even take time to prayerfully write it out. What led you to decide to follow Jesus? What was your life like before? After? Do not glorify sin, but glorify Jesus. What has changed in your heart? Again, you can do this in as little as 30 seconds, or you can take 20 minutes or an hour.

Six: *Pray for people on the spot.* I love asking, "What would you like for Jesus to do for you?" -- and really listening to the answer and engaging with them, and then praying in faith. Take time to pause and be still before God. Focus on Jesus. Seek to become aware of the presence of God and pray for the other person to experience it too. Touch them if it's appropriate. Believe that what you are asking will come to pass for the glory of His Name.

Seven: *Trust in the life-giving power of the Holy Spirit.* This is a spiritual work. You cannot convince or talk someone into following Jesus. Trust that the Spirit of God is at work, doing what you cannot do. Depend on Him. Go in weakness; even as a fool.

I have to confess to you that sharing the Gospel is not easy for me. I struggle to do it, even in situations where there is an obvious open door. I wish I was not so weak in this area. My heart longs to be a bold and powerful witness for Jesus, but I miss so many opportunities. Sometimes I am content to excuse myself, easing my mind with the thought that it's just not my personality or my gifting to evangelize. But I know better. By His grace, when I do step out, He is there. He truly does help. God does not expect you to be a rock star evangelist. He just wants you to share the amazing Good News that has the power to change everything. Being weak is ok.

"When I came to you, brothers, I did not come with eloquence or superior wisdom as I proclaimed to you the testimony about God. For I resolved to know nothing while I was with you except Jesus Christ and him crucified. I came to you in weakness and fear, and with much trembling." – 1 Corinthians 2:1-3

You can do that! You can just focus on Jesus and talk about Him and make it all about Him. And you can be weak. You might even be afraid. Praise God! You're another Paul! Go for it!

9 THE POOR
What Are We to Do?

Have you ever heard it said that we find Jesus in the face of the poor? I think I read something like that in a story about Mother Theresa. Inspired, I wanted to experience the same thing – or at least to be able to have something cool and profound to tell. But in going to talk to a poor man, he only begged money from me, and I was offended. In inviting a poor child into my yard to play with my kids, he stole from us, and I was angry. And, in hopes of catching a glimpse of Jesus in a poor baby, she peed on me, and I was wet. And I smelled bad. Maybe I was with the wrong poor? Or maybe there's something wrong with the eyes of my heart.

King Jehoiakim was a wicked king of Judah, placed on the throne by the Egyptians. God spoke His judgment against him through the prophet Jeremiah, and in so doing, compared him to his righteous father, Josiah. God says that Josiah

"...helped those who were poor and needy, so everything went well for him. That is what it means to know God,' says the LORD." Jeremiah 22:16

Wow. Helping the poor and needy is what it means to know God. In the New Testament, James makes a similar claim:

"Religion that God accepts as pure and without fault is this: caring for orphans or widows who need help, and keeping yourself free from the world's evil influence." James 1:27

Clearly, our relationship with God is not complete without caring for the poor. (Did someone say 'Yikes?') Similarly, Jesus says that when we help the poor, we are actually helping Him:

"Then these righteous ones will reply, 'Lord, when did we ever see you hungry and feed you? Or thirsty and give you something to drink? Or a stranger and show you hospitality? Or naked and give you clothing? When did we ever see you sick or in prison, and visit you?' And the King will tell them, 'I assure you, when you did it to one of the least of these my brothers and sisters, you were doing it to me!'" -- Matthew 25:37-40

In the subsequent verses of that passage, He makes it clear that the opposite is also true: refusing help to the needy is the same as refusing Him.

Helping the poor is one of those things that sounds wonderfully lofty, but, as I mentioned at the beginning, does not often feel that way in the midst of actually trying to do it. It is something that always inspires in speeches by Bono and in books about Francis of Assisi and in articles and blogs by anybody. But the reality is that it's one thing to lobby on behalf of the poor and to applaud those who fight for the poor, but to actually do something myself is another thing altogether. It's hard. And yet the Bible is clear that our relationship with God cannot be separated from this issue. Jesus really is there with the poor, and if we want to be where

He is, we've got to get there too. Eventually, following Jesus must lead us to that part of the world or that part of town we've always avoided in the past.

I believe we have to get this into our heads: there is a special place in God's heart for the poor and for the oppressed and for the outcasts. For widows and for orphans. For refugees. Yes, the Gospel is for all. Yes, He loves me in a special way. But there is something to this idea that even a casual reading of scripture clearly reveals. The poor are special to God. His heart goes out to them. He defends them and cares for them. He likes to be with them. Incredibly, He identifies with them. And yes, He calls us to do the same.

I have to say this: *Sooner or later, you are going to have to deal with the American worship of money.* "You cannot serve both God and Money" (Matthew 6:24). Money is an idol in our country, and the chances are that the worship of it has had some impact on you. Ask God to show you your own heart.

"Search me, O God, and know my heart; test me and know my anxious thoughts.

See if there is any offensive way in me, and lead me in the way everlasting." -- Psalm 139:23-24

Ask Him to reveal any idol that might be there. Is money your security? Do you count on it to bring happiness? Is it easy for you to part with it? Are you content with what you have, or do you need more? One great way to fight the love of money is to learn the secret of contentment.

"I know what it is to be in need, and I know what it is to have plenty. I have learned the secret of being content in any and every situation, whether well fed or hungry, whether living in plenty or in want. I can do everything through him who gives me strength."- Philippians 4:12-13

"But godliness with contentment is great gain. For we brought nothing into the world, and we can take nothing out of it. But if we have food and clothing, we will be content with that. People who want to get rich fall into temptation and a trap and into many foolish and harmful desires that plunge men into ruin and destruction. For the love of money is a root of all kinds of evil. Some people, eager for money, have wandered from the faith and pierced themselves with many griefs." - 1 Timothy 6:6-10

So what do we do with this? What can you do? Here are some ideas that may help us to serve among the poor in a Christ-like manner:

First, *look for Jesus among the poor.* In spite of the all-too-common experiences I mentioned at the outset, this is really a great place to start. However, let me just say that it matters how we look, and what our expectations are. Do not be out for a profound mystical encounter. There is nothing mystical about pee-pee. Do not look for a feel-good experience. You may say, "Oh, it's just so fulfilling to be able to help them." Until you get conned. Finding Jesus among the poor might have as much to do with changing what we expect Jesus to look like as it does changing the way we look at the poor. Actually, one probably leads to the other. Finding Jesus among people does not mean that they have to be nice. Or clean. Or Christian. Or honest. It does not even mean that they give a rip about you or your God. But He is still there. I don't really get it. It's not that He is in the meanness or the lying or greed. But He is there because this is who He came for. He loves them. He is close to them. He is pursuing and wooing them.

"The Spirit of the Lord is on me,
    because he has anointed me to preach good
    news to the poor." Luke 4:18

Secondly, *be generous.* I believe God loves it when His people show concern for people in need in practical ways. Be willing and ready to give. Give sacrificially. 2 Corinthians 8-9 is all about giving generously to help the poor. Give it a read. Here's how it begins:

"And now, brothers, we want you to know about the grace that God gave the Macedonian churches. Out of the most severe trial, their overflowing joy and their extreme poverty welled up in rich generosity. For I testify that they gave as much as they were able and beyond their ability." 2 Corinthians 8:1-3

Thirdly, *honor and seek to know the one to whom you give.* Shane Claiborne said this: "The great tragedy in the church is not that rich Christians do not care about the poor, but that rich Christians do not know the poor."[10] Give yourself. Spend a little time with the person to whom you want to give. Get to know each other. Be a friend. Touch him. Pray for him. Talk to him as an equal. Understand that, although you have a lot more money than him, we're all rich in some ways and poor in others. Do not in your pity look down on him or feel superior to him. It is no use protesting to me that you wouldn't do that. It's a natural reaction, and you will have to deal with it. Fight it. Do not patronize. Recognize the dignity and value that is in the person as one created in the image of God, and one for whom Jesus died.

---

[10] Shane Claiborne, p 113.

Understand that your generosity often carries with it very subtle but nonetheless significant issues of power. This is especially the case when you do not have a significant relationship with the person helped before you give to them – obviously a common circumstance in short-term missions. When you are just getting to know the people to whom you give, your connection with them becomes largely defined by the giving. Built into the very foundation of the relationship is the fact that you gave to them. Now you in some way have an upper hand. They begin to develop the need to please you. They feel pressure to use the money in a way that will make you happy. They must report to you for the purpose of "accountability." Maybe you do not intend it to be this way, but you can certainly communicate this kind of attitude even without knowing it – and even if you don't communicate it at all, it can be assumed, and often is. So what to do? For now, just think it through, and be aware.

Fourthly, *Find out what they truly want and need.* Many people travel to rural Africa and think, "if these people just had a toilet like ours they'd be so much happier." Just because we are uncomfortable using their toilets does not mean that they are. "Wow, they don't even have running water. They're even worse off than I thought!" This comment was made several years ago by a missionary about an African pastor who is a friend of mine, and it represents a common misconception. This pastor was actually pretty well off – not exactly wealthy, but certainly comfortable middle-class. He owned a nice, well furnished house and a nice car. His children – all six of them – went to good schools. He often traveled internationally. He was a business owner with a number of employees working for him. Running water was just not a priority for him and his family. It is a luxury item that perhaps one day they will have, but it's nowhere near the top of the list of wants or needs. Missionaries have been trying to improve people's lives for a long time, and that is very good. But sometimes we are more than a little bit arrogant in the way we go about it. One experienced short-term missionary makes the point that, "Our financial wealth, and all the amenities that accompany that, easily inclines us to think that we know what these people need."[11] In fact, we do not.

Fifthly, *follow the directions of your leaders and contacts.* It is good to give. But sometimes there is a good way to give and a not-so-good way to give. Let's give in a good way. The best way to ensure this is to go through your leaders. Tell them it is on your heart to give to a certain person or ministry and ask the best way to go about it. It may be that you will be advised to think long term. It might feel great to you to give some money or food or a gift to an orphan that you have been playing with, but something else might be much more helpful. Maybe your host would challenge you to support the child with $25 every month instead, or give money to buy a pair of shoes, or pay school fees for one term. You want to help, so why not be sure that you really are? Follow compassion when you feel compelled to give, but do not just do something for the sake of making *you* feel better.

Does it really say that?
The scriptures have a lot to say about the poor. Spend some time studying the following passages and look for more:
"Defend the weak and the fatherless; uphold the cause of the poor and the oppressed." Psalm 82:3

---

[11] David Livermore, p 53.

"Whoever oppresses the poor shows contempt for their Maker, but whoever is kind to the needy honors God." Proverbs 14:31

"Whoever is kind to the poor lends to the LORD, and he will reward them for what they have done." Proverbs 19:17

"Share your food with the hungry and bring poor, homeless people into your own homes. When you see someone who has no clothes, give him yours, and don't refuse to help your own relatives." Isaiah 58:7 (NCV)

"A brother of sister in Christ might need clothes or food. If you say to that person, 'God be with you! I hope you stay warm and get plenty to eat,' but you do not give what that person needs, your words are worth nothing." James 2:15-16 (NCV)

"Suppose someone has enough to live and sees a brother or sister in need, but does not help. Then God's love is not living in that person." 1 John 3:17 (NCV)

Have you ever seriously considered these words of Jesus?

"Then Jesus said to the man who had invited him, 'When you give a lunch or a dinner, don't invite only your friends, your family, your other relatives, and your rich neighbors. At another time they will invite you to eat with them, and you will be repaid. Instead, when you give a feast, invite the poor, the crippled, the lame, and the blind. Then you will be blessed, because they have nothing and cannot pay you back. But you will be repaid when the good people rise from the dead.'" Luke 14:12-14 (NCV)

When Jesus was beginning His public ministry, and stating who He is and what He came to do, He quoted from the prophet Isaiah:
> "The Spirit of the Lord is on me,
> because he has anointed me to preach good news to the poor.
> He has sent me to proclaim freedom for the prisoners and recovery of sight for the blind,
> to release the oppressed, to proclaim the year of the Lord's favor." Luke 4:18-19

Yes, Jesus loves the poor. It's about time we do too.

10 SIMULATOR

A missionary friend told me a true story about someone coming from another country for a short visit to America. While in Houston, he was taken to learn about the space program, and had the opportunity to experience a simulator that gave a little of the feel of what it's like going in a space ship to the Moon. He could see out the windows and feel the thrust of the engines. Upon returning to his home, a group of people came over to visit and hear about his trip to America. He told them about how he had been given the chance to go to the Moon. His audience was astonished, to say the least. One person dared to ask if he was really sure he actually went, or perhaps he was in a machine that made him feel like he went. "I tell you, I went to the Moon. I went to the Moon. I was there. I experienced it!" was his unwavering reply. He wasn't lying -- he really thought he had gone, and he will never be convinced otherwise.

Some people are convinced that they are doing mission work of some kind, but in reality they are just in a simulator. They are having an experience that approximates genuine mission and outreach, but in fact is not. I know that you really did get on the plane and you really did leave the United States. Or you really do drive across town once a week. But missions? Not necessarily. It is only missions if you are truly there on

Jesus' mission, in Jesus' way. Are you leaving an imprint of Jesus where you go? Are you revealing His glory? Jesus' mission was and is to seek and to save the lost.

That was His mission -- and this is how He did it: John 1:14 says

"The Word became flesh and made his dwelling among us. We have seen His glory, the glory of the One and Only, who came from the Father, full of grace and truth."

People saw the glory of God when Jesus looked like the folks He came to save. Don't miss this. Jesus took on flesh and they saw the glory of God. You'll not reveal the glory of Jesus unless you take a similar approach. Do all you can to identify with the people you are there to reach. Fight past the cultural strangeness, the language barrier, and everything that makes you different. Look into the heart.

Do not form a clique with your team. You are not going for the sake of your team, but for the lost. This is tough. It is natural to develop incredibly tight and rewarding relationships with the people who are going through this experience with you. And this is good. You will need your teammates, and their friendship can be something that truly enlarges your ministry. But remember why you are out there. Be a team for the sake of the people you are sent to reach -- across the world or on the other side of town. Learn to depend on the locals, to trust them, to relate to them.

Think about Jesus' incarnation, especially the glory that He left behind and how fully He identified with the people He came to reach. Hebrews 4:15 says this about Jesus (in the Message):

"We don't have a priest who is out of touch with our reality. He's been through weakness and testing, experienced it all — all but the sin."

One of the most devastating mistakes we can make as missionaries is to be "out of touch with [their] reality." We have the message. We have the truth and the power – but it is not being received. It is not even being understood. Why is this? We're out of touch. We speak without listening. We teach without learning. We give without receiving. We "minister" without serving. We have no clue. *Learn to need the people you've come to serve.*

I want to encourage you to jump into this new culture with enthusiasm and a sense of adventure. You may not see how entering someone's home or drinking the tea they serve you or learning how to greet in their language can help you to fulfill your mission, but it will. You are taking on their flesh. You are beginning to experience life a little bit from their perspective and making an attempt to see the world through their eyes. This is huge. You are becoming less of an angel descending from the sky with a message and more a miniature incarnation – bringing the power and the glory and the love of Jesus in the form of a flesh and blood fellow human. It is powerful. I am so challenged by the example of Paul in this, when he told the Thessalonians:

"We loved you so much that we were delighted to share with you not only the gospel of God but our lives as well, because you had become so dear to us" (1 Thess 2:8).

Wow! Do you think we would be able to write this about our mission outreach? Can you give not only the Gospel of God, but your lives as well?

"Even though I am free of the demands and expectations of everyone, I have voluntarily become a servant to any and all in order to reach a wide range of people: religious, nonreligious, meticulous moralists, loose-living immoralists, the defeated, the demoralized—whoever. I didn't take on their way of life. I kept my bearings in Christ—but entered their world and tried to experience things from their point of view. I've become just about every sort of servant there is in my attempts to lead those I meet into a God-saved life. I did all this because of the Message. I didn't just want to talk about it; I wanted to be in on it!" -- 1 Corinthians 9:19-23 (MSG)

Do this, and I believe they will see the glory of God as He reveals Himself through your flesh. That is real missions.

As a missionary living in Uganda, I often cringed at the comments made by fellow-missionaries – and sometimes by myself. Looking back I feel sick. In these comments, missionaries would often refer to Ugandans as "*them*" or "*they*." And of course, Westerners would be included in "*us*" or "*we*." It is the same in Tulsa, OK. The homeless are the *thems*, and the middle class are the *us's*.

Cultural pride is a natural part of human nature. We automatically assume that certain ways of doing things are superior to other ways. It is better to be on time than to be late. It is better to work very hard all the time than to visit with a friend. It is better to get the job done as efficiently as possible. It is better to do everything with "excellence," no matter what. It is better to drive on the right side of the road than the left. Such assumptions work well in your culture, but they may not necessarily be the prevailing way of thinking among other peoples. When we go as missionaries, it is up to us to adapt to the culture we are wanting to reach with the Gospel. But how, in a few short days, can I become able to truly communicate and relate in this new culture? If we are so different on so many levels, how can I hope to be effective as a short-term missionary? Even in my own city, how can I relate to those who are so different from me?

When I first went to Africa, I was honestly paranoid about offending the culture. I'd heard too many lectures about "ugly Americans." I therefore would sit quietly in the bus and never speak above a whisper. *Oh man, is it ok to cross my legs? Did I make an offensive gesture? Is it bad to scratch my elbow?* It was ridiculous, and I was unable to be an effective witness because I wasn't free. This is not necessary. We do not have to be an expert of a culture before entering it. It is good to study beforehand, but I've found that our attitude is much more important than our knowledge. I believe there are four successive roles we can take on that will enable us to break through into any culture, whether at home or abroad. If you determine in your heart to go as this kind of person, you will be able to make meaningful connections in a short period of time.[12]

The first role is that of a *learner*. Be a student of the culture. Ask questions of everyone. "How do you..." prepare dinner or buy a cow or make passion fruit juice or get married or get a job or make a friend or get your hair cut or make an appointment or treat a fever? Or "why do you..." do it like that or say it that way or whatever. What kind of government do you have? Is it a good one? What are your schools like?

---

[12] These roles are adapted from Thomas Brewster's "learner-servant-storyteller" model. This in turn was an adaptation of Donald Larson's "learner-trader-storyteller." See *Language Learning is Communication is Ministry* by E. Thomas Brewster and Elizabeth S. Brewster (Pasadena: Lingua House, 1984), pgs 11-15. I highly recommend this small booklet.

Did you like school? Why do those coffins have windows? Does that thing on his head have any significance? Why aren't you smiling in that photo? What's your favorite food? How do you make it? What kind of tree is that? What's your favorite thing to do? Do you play games? Learn! Let everyone know that this person is interested in us.

As you are establishing yourself as a learner, seek to become a *servant*. Do not stop learning even a little bit, but add this role. Sometimes this can be tricky, especially if you are in a culture that honors visitors and does not want to let you do anything for them. But persist (in a sensitive way). Show a willingness to do anything. To get dirty. To sweat. To spend time. Hold a baby. Lay out a mat. Pour some tea. Carry a load. Clean up a mess. Sometimes there's nothing you can practically do – especially in a short encounter. But your attitude can come through even so. Show respect to each person. *"In humility consider others better than yourselves"* (Philippians 2:3).

Show honor to the leaders whose ministry you are coming to help. Sometimes Americans have the reputation for coming into a place as know-it-alls, ready to correct and "fix" everything. Remember, you are in this country to help those who live and serve the Lord here. God has graciously allowed you to come and participate in His ministry with His people. Sometimes we act as though this is our project or our ministry, and we're inviting local leaders to come and be involved with what we are doing. No way! We're thankful to get involved in what God is doing through them!

"Whoever wants to become great among you must be your servant, and whoever wants to be first must be your slave – just as the Son of Man did not come to be served,

but to serve, and to give his life as a ransom for many."
Matthew 20:26-28

"Now that I, your Lord and Teacher, have washed your feet, you also should wash one another's feet. I have set you an example that you should do as I have done for you." John 13:15-15

One of the most amazing things that can happen on a missions trip is that you can become a *friend*. As you learn and serve, still be yourself. Your quietness or your craziness or your seriousness or your humor or your love of basketball or babies or books or bananas are all part of who you are. Share this with the people you come into contact with. If you're a joker, joke around with people (while being culturally sensitive). If you love deep conversations, engage in them with nationals. If you play games, ask your new acquaintances to teach you local ones. Enjoy people. Get to know what they are like. Show genuine interest in their families and their hopes and fears and dreams. Share yours, too. Open up a little. Or a lot. People are interesting. God created each one, and they are so different yet so alike. All of us have an imprint of God's image. We've smudged it a lot, but it's there. Be wowed by people. Be captivated by them.

Take this challenge – make at least one good friend among the nationals in the country where you are going. If you are involved in a local ministry in your own city, do the same. Become genuine friends with someone to whom you are ministering. This could be a pastor, an interpreter, someone in the local church, a homeless man, a little child, a builder, someone you witnessed to, a hotel worker, a shopkeeper, a student, an orphan, a beggar. Whoever. Begin praying now, and ask the Lord to lead you and connect you. Let this person be your teacher. Talk about your hopes and dreams, and listen to your friend's.

Finally, be a *story-teller*. You have the most wonderful story to tell! You have a message to share! Do it. Through your learning, your servanthood, and your friendship, you are opening doors to speak into people's lives. You've heard their story, and they are almost certainly interested in yours. Tell them about Jesus. Tell them what He has meant to you. Tell them how they can know Him and follow Him too, and how He died to give them eternal life. Use all that you've learned about the culture and the individual person to make the message understandable and to show how it fits. Share your testimony. Share about your life. Exalt Jesus and reveal Him in a clear and loving way.

Culture can hinder our message and render us unfruitful – but only if we insist on blundering ahead in ignorance. On the other hand, culture can be a beautiful thing, and an aid in sharing the Gospel. Find God's hand in it. Appreciate it. Enjoy it.

11 LONELY PLACES

I need quiet time with the Lord each day in order to make it. I really do. Not to be saved. Not to be loved by the Father. But to actually be aware of His love, to trust in Him, to represent Him well. And my guess is that you do as well. For much of my Christian life, I thought this whole idea was a real drag. Something probably important in a theoretical, nebulous kind of way, but not exactly energizing. A trip to the dentist for a check-up. Getting the oil changed in my car. A necessary nuisance. In fact, it's been such a struggle for me over the years that I feel somewhat hypocritical in writing about it. The truth is, I used to hate the idea of having to get up early and try to pray and read the Bible every single day. To be fair, there were occasions when I sort of liked it. There were seasons when it was better, and I would walk in the realization of how much I needed it.

When my wife and I went to Africa as missionaries, we served under a ministry that required us to sign a statement saying we would spend at least an hour in personal prayer and Bible study every day. When we first arrived in Uganda, it was incredible. I lived with such a constant awareness of my need for help from heaven that the hour-a-day was no problem at all. I was being assaulted by all kinds of stuff that was so new to me, and I was desperate for God. But as the months and then years went by, I got more comfortable. I lost the desperation. Horrible pangs of guilt would strike me once every year when we opened the mail and found the dreaded document from our mission – the renewal of the prayer covenant. Guilt. My devotional life could be summarized with a few words: Inconsistent. Guilt. Bland. Yes, I'd sign the repulsive form – with genuine repentance and determination to do better. It never lasted.

In Africa, I used to go on mission trips with my Ugandan fellow-workers from time to time. It was crazy. Inevitably, after experiencing a restless few hours of sleep because of the newness of the place, the fear of rats, or whatever, I'd hear the infuriating sound. My friends would be up praying. And do not think this was a 'quiet time.' Oh no. This was serious spiritual warfare, binding demons, crying out to God, singing, worshiping, intense, fervent, passionate prayer. I'd look at my clock (*4:00 in the freakin morning!*) groan, roll over, put whatever was serving as my pillow over my head, and try to get back to blissful slumber. I was annoyed. I'd eventually fade back out, only to wake up several hours later with that familiar companion rubbing it in – *guilt*.

Oh, but please listen to me! Prayer is a beautiful gift to you from your Creator. The Bible is an incomparable treasure. And you desperately need to spend time with Jesus each day. You know it with your head. You've heard it dozens of times. You've told others. You agree with me. But have you grasped it in the deep part of your heart? It is *true*! You need this. Jesus Himself clearly prioritized prayer. He was always trying to get away to hang with His Father.

> "Very early in the morning, while it was still dark, Jesus got up, left the house and went off to a solitary place, where he prayed." Mark 1:35

"But Jesus often withdrew to lonely places and prayed."
Luke 5:16

"One of those days Jesus went out to a mountainside to
pray, and spent the night praying to God." Luke 6:12

"About eight days after Jesus said this, he took Peter, John
and James with him and went up onto a mountain to
pray." Luke 9:28

"One day Jesus was praying in a certain place. When he
finished, one of his disciples said to him, 'Lord, teach us to
pray, just as John taught his disciples.'" Luke 11:1

"They went to a place called Gethsemane, and Jesus said
to his disciples, "Sit here while I pray.'" Mark 14:32

God calls us to pray and read the Bible and fast and
worship and all that stuff for a reason. It is not meant to be a
burden or to constantly wear us down with guilt. It is because
we need it. I have a passion within me to know Jesus and to
make Him known, to live for Him and His glory. It burns in
my heart. I really believe I would do anything to bring it
about. But I know this from experience: passions can fade.
They can lose their heat. I do not want to lose this passion, so
I must feed it. I have to fan it into flame.
"This is why I remind you to fan into flames the spiritual
gift God gave you when I laid my hands on you." 2
Timothy 1:6 (NLT)

There's some stuff that we need to fight to keep. Our passion for Jesus is one of them. Our desire for His glory. Our determination for our lives to count for Him. Our longing for His Kingdom to come.

"Seek the Kingdom of God above all else, and live righteously, and he will give you everything you need."
Matthew 6:33 (NLT)

Seek it. Fan it into flame. That's why all this stuff – what we sometimes call spiritual disciplines – is so important. It's how we fan the flame, seek the Kingdom, feed the passion. This is one of the secrets to maintaining steady, guilt-free, sweet quiet times with the Lord – to know why we're doing it. We are doing it because we love Him and we want to know Him. We need it to live lives worthy of Him and to keep the godly passions ablaze in our hearts.

Sometimes we find ourselves in a place where we simply do not have space. We live in a small dorm room with a roommate or two. We're on a missions trip and never have a single moment alone. Jesus' time away in "lonely places" seems like an extravagant luxury. What can one do? Well, be creative. Learn to pray in your head. Write your prayers. Put on head phones and listen to worship music on your bed. Read your Bible and meditate even with stuff going on all around. It is not ideal in a sense, but it is still possible. If you're motivated, you can find a way. Here are a few other ideas as to how to maintain a quiet time:

1   *Be accountable.* Talk to a friend, and agree to help one another to spend time with the Lord. Maybe this could be your roommate, or another person who is part of your outreach. It could be one of your leaders. Wake each other up. Ask each other how it went. Encourage and

exhort one another. *Do not* make excuses for each other. Spur one another on!

2   *Pray according to the pattern Jesus taught* in Matthew 6:9-13. This could be an in-depth teaching in itself, but briefly it could broken down like this:

✦ *Our Father in heaven, hallowed be thy name.* Approach God as your Father. Meditate on this. And then worship Him. Lay your life before Him as a living sacrifice (Rom 12:1).

✦ *Your kingdom come, your will be done on earth as it is in heaven.* Surrender yourself to God's will today. Commit yourself to pursuing what he wants. In praying for His kingdom to come, intercede for others. Pray for the lost. For your outreach, or the nation where you are serving. Your team. Your loved ones. This is spiritual warfare. Be fervent!

✦ *Give us today our daily bread.* Make your requests known to God. He invites you to ask for what you need.

✦ *Forgive us our sins, as we also have forgiven those who have sinned against us.* Ask the Lord to reveal your sins to you, and repent of them one by one. Also consciously forgive anyone who has offended you.

✦ *And lead us not into temptation but deliver us from the evil one.* Ask for help to overcome sin today. You know the areas where you are likely to struggle. Get help from heaven! Also pray against every scheme and attack of the enemy.

✦ *For yours is the kingdom, the power, and the glory forever. Amen.* End with declaring and reminding yourself that it is all His, and all about Him.

Do this as a pattern, but be sensitive to the Holy Spirit. Do not let your time with Jesus denigrate into a business meeting. Be flexible and spontaneous as well. Use the form, but do not get stuck in it.

3 *Pray in response to reading the Bible.* Read a passage, and pray back to God as you read. Develop a conversation with Him in this way. Talk to Him as you listen for His voice speaking to you through the Bible. This can be fun!

4 *Journal.* A prayer journal has been a terrific help in my quiet times. I pray and read the Bible, but I also take time to write out what's happening within me. I often do this as a prayer, but it is always a different experience than a spoken prayer. I write about what is bothering me or what I'm excited about or what I'm learning. I love to write what I sense God may be speaking to me, and what He has been teaching me through a sermon or an experience or the Bible or another person or simply from His Spirit speaking in my heart. I love this.

5 *Focus on grace, not guilt.* Receive God's grace when you fail. When you miss a day or two. Or a week or two. When you do pray but you don't believe, or you do read the Bible but you don't focus. This is not a duty. It is not

something God requires of you just because. This is your food. You do not beat yourself up if you miss breakfast. It just makes you extra ready for lunch. Be motivated by hunger, not guilt.

6   *Get inspired.* Read books about prayer. Listen to podcasts. Find things that motivate and encourage you in prayer. Fan the flame.

7   *Mix it up.* Go on a walk. Visit a prayer room. Take your Bible and journal to a favorite coffee shop. Go for a bike ride. Use a prayer book. You don't have to do the same thing every day. Be creative and have fun!

8   *Ask God to help you.* He wants to help you in this. He wants to spend quality time with you. He wants to abide with you. Keep asking Him. Do not give up. He will increase your desire.

12 EMILY'S STORY

It should have been a normal missions trip -- serve for a week and then come home to "real" life. Like thousands of other college students, Emily was giving up part of her break to follow Jesus in serving the poor and proclaiming the Gospel. There was nothing particularly special or impressive about the location. Just across the border in Mexico, Reynosa is not a place that people tend to get excited about. A dead end town. Nor was Emily's ministry there that Spring Break especially noteworthy. In fact, she was scrubbing the floor behind a crack bar when it happened. God spoke to her, and in a moment she saw her life from a very different perspective. The ups and downs of college life -- the stresses and the pleasures, the ambitions and anxieties -- all seemed to fade. And this place, this forgotten, dirty, unimpressive place... And these people, these prostitutes and pimps and addicts... All of it suddenly became extremely significant. She would give her life for Jesus in this town, for these people.

And so it began. From that day, Emily entered a journey that she would never have imagined, and along the way faced trials for which she would never have knowingly signed up. Yet in all of it -- in all the bitter disappointments and confusing moments, all the experiences of sheer terror and deep hurt -- she knew it was worth it. That moment scrubbing the floor of a prostitute's bar had given her Heaven's eyes through which to see the world, and nothing could be the same.

After graduating from college, Emily attended language school to learn Spanish, and then moved to be part of a 24-7 Prayer team serving in Reynosa. Specifically, this team was targeting the infamous "Boys Town" -- a place of legalized prostitution and drugs run by the Mexican mafia. Emily and the team she joined would spend hours walking the streets and praying, interceding for the entrapped women selling their bodies, the hollow men always willing to buy anything that might fill the void, and the love-starved youth running drugs for the violent and greedy lords of the city. They prayed with groans and with tears and with desperation. Sometimes they managed to pray in faith. Often it was all they could do to simply ward off despair.

In addition to prayer, Emily's primary ministry may have been throwing parties. As time went on, she became friends with a number of the prostitutes who lived in this "zone of tolerance." Her deep desire was to communicate value to these women and girls who knew such unbearable hurt and rejection. So on their birthdays, she would bake some goodies, gather friends, and celebrate a life. She would tell the surprised girls that they had value because they were known and loved by a Father in heaven, unlike any person they had ever encountered. She would tell them and show them that they were worth celebrating. That they could be loved. That they were not too dirty or too marred or too used.

She never really knew if her message got through. There was so much to overcome. So much reality to walk through. But she and her friends persisted. They prayed. They were present. They listened. They valued. They spoke Gospel words. They partied. And they prayed some more.

Suddenly, almost against her will, Emily found herself back "home" in Tulsa. Circumstances had spun out of control. The city was reeling. Her team dispersed. Alone, she couldn't go back -- and yet how could she abandon her friends? Thus began years of questioning and praying and seeking and striving to hold onto old hopes and resurrect dead dreams. Seemingly within a few breaths, Emily went from creating birthday parties in brothels to crafting high-priced lattes for businessmen. From weeping in the dirty streets of Boys Town to living in a comfortable and safe apartment in Tulsa. "Home" was harder to take than the "mission field."

In time, Emily simply went back to what she knew. Continuing to pray and intercede for Boys Town from Tulsa, she began asking the Lord to send her back. Slowly, He opened doors. Her story inspired friends, and her passion moved them. She took a trip to serve a team as interpreter and helper. Later, she led a church team back to pray and re-engage friendships. I was on this team, and the experience marked my life. We walked and prayed and celebrated and wept on those dusty streets that Emily knew so well. We met Blanca. Emily had known Blanca for years as an aging prostitute, hopeless addict, and belligerent presence. But... in the time that Emily had been gone from Reynosa, Blanca had encountered Jesus and been truly born again. She was new, and was beyond excited to tell Emily of her transformed life. Oh the goodness of the Father! In Blanca we encountered tangible fruit, produced out of those years of intercession and parties and pleading. Blanca and Emily rejoiced together in tears as they recounted the old days and began to dream together of the years ahead.

There have been more trips and more prayer and more giving and more planning and scheming. Emily has taken numerous people on prayer journeys to Reynosa, and has managed to maintain some key relationships. Through her, our church is able to send one precious girl, born in Boys Town, to school -- where she has hope for a different life than her mother and grandmother have known.

Emily's story is not a neat and clean one. It has taken many turns, and encountered too many unforeseen obstacles to mention. The end is still not known, and Emily's future with Reynosa is still up in the air. Life can be like that. But this is what I want to pass on to you: as you serve on a missions trip or in your city, be open. Allow Jesus to change the way you see the world. Invite Him to overhaul your value system and to wreck your little plans. Surrender to His gently persistent call. Ask Him to move your heart with the things that move His. Be ready to cancel your plans and exchange your ambitions. Don't expect the way to be easy or clear or smooth. You may be led through mists of confusion and challenges you would never desire. But, as Emily would tell you, it's worth it.

13 WAR OF THE SPIRIT

"Finally, be strong in the Lord and in His mighty power. Put on the full armor of God, so that you can take your stand against the devil's schemes. For our struggle is not against flesh and blood, but against the rulers, against the authorities, against the powers of this dark world and against the spiritual forces of evil in the heavenly realms. Therefore put on the full armor of God, so that when the day of evil comes, you may be able to stand your ground, and after you have done everything, to stand." -- Ephesians 6:10-13.

I love the book of Ephesians. It paints such a glorious and epic picture of the Church. It lays out the amazing things that Jesus has done for us -- adopting us, forgiving us, unifying us, making us belong, providing good works for us to do. We are told that we are a new humanity. That we (the Church) make known the wisdom and power of God to the powers. We have a great and lofty purpose with cosmic implications. We are deeply loved, and can actually experience that love. We are part of God's family. We have a key role in the Father's plan to bring redemption to the world. We have gifts, and our gifts are needed for His body to be fully mature. All seems bright and beautiful. Ever-increasing glory.

But then we come to this last little section of the letter, and, seemingly out of nowhere, things turn darkly sinister. The metaphors shift from bride to warrior; from son to soldier. Suddenly we're faced with a malicious enemy, flaming arrows, and a deathly struggle to simply stand. We encounter spiritual forces arrayed against us; Undefined entities of apparently great craftiness and power. Shadowy, spooky images of spirit-beings and evil days. What happened?! Where did this come from?

The Old Testament stories of the conquest of the Promised Land provide a clue as to what is happening here. God told generations of Abraham's family that the land was theirs. He had decreed it so and given it to them. Finally, after more than four centuries, the time was right, and He announced to the Patriarch's enslaved descendants that it was time to claim the promise. What happened next is the confusing part. God had given them the land. But there were enemies there. They had to fight to receive it. Of course, God would fight for them, but they still had to put on their armor, grab their weapons, line up for battle, and engage the enemy. The victory was secure as long as they trusted in God. But they still had to fight. They suffered losses and experienced painful defeats. Sometimes they failed to obey the Lord and the consequences were disastrous. Even in the victories, they almost always had to participate in the violent struggle. They were bloodied and bruised and exhausted. Some died. They were frightened and overwhelmed. But, as long as they stood firm and trusted the Lord, they would advance.

And that brings us back to Ephesians 6 and the warfare of the Spirit. All the wonderful promises of the previous chapters are ours. They have been given to us by our loving and powerful God. But we still have an enemy and we still have to stand. We still need to believe and we still will suffer losses. We will be bloodied and bruised, exhausted and overwhelmed. Like the Israelites of old, our enemy is too strong for us, and we cannot hope to survive apart from the mighty power of our God.

As you engage lost and hurting people with the intention of rescuing them from the darkness that has them bound, you will face a determined foe. In the struggle for people's lives and freedom, you will encounter disappointment. The sick will remain in their infirmity. The broken will persist in their destructive habits. The poor will continue to be overwhelmed. In the context of all this, your prayers will seem unanswered, your words powerless, and all your efforts inconsequential. But have faith. *Have faith!* Stand in the midst of the fray unwavering. Jesus is at work. You cannot see it yet, but He calls you to persevere.

"Therefore, my dear brothers and sisters, stand firm. Let nothing move you. Always give yourselves fully to the work of the Lord, because you know that your labor in the Lord is not in vain." -- 1 Corinthians 15:58

We need God's power to stand in the face of the onslaught. And make no mistake; He makes that mighty power available to us. And this is how that power is wielded -- through truth, righteousness, the Gospel, salvation, faith, His Word, and prayer. See Ephesians 6:13-18.

Believing God is an act of war. The devil is taking aim at you. Faith is your shield. You have suffered some hits. You have realized that things do not always go well. You have been confused by injustice or seemingly unanswered prayer or depression or failure or death or simply boredom.

76

I think of such times in my life and I am grateful for the mighty power of God to enable me to simply stand when even that was far beyond me. Some of you are there now. And I can tell you, and urge you, and encourage you: *Have faith!* God is not as absent as you feel He is. He has not forgotten you or those you love. He has not turned mean or cruel. He is with you. And you must believe it.

"And it is impossible to please God without faith. Anyone who wants to come to him must believe that God exists and that he rewards those who sincerely seek him." -- Hebrews 11:6

Do not worry. He understands your doubts. He will work with you. He will respond to your honesty and your reality.

"I do believe, but help me overcome my unbelief!" -- Mark 9:24

But He is not content for you to stay there. He demands that we believe; that we have faith. His most common rebuke of the Twelve was about their lack of faith. He urged them to believe. Believing is how we stand.

But what if I don't?

Live like you do. Ultimately, faith is more of a decision than a feeling. You may feel doubt, but you can still live by faith. Yes, I understand that is hard; But it is your path to life. Probably the biggest way to fight this battle of faith is by doing all the seemingly insignificant things Paul lays out in Ephesians 4-6. Not using profane or degrading or crude language, but instead encouraging people and being thankful. Forgiving. Not giving into sexual immorality, but being intensely pure. Not wallowing in bitterness or anger, but forgiving and letting go. Submitting to one another. Loving your wife and not exasperating your kids. Respecting your husband. Working hard and sharing with those in need. How do you live by faith? You pray. You read the Word. You act and think and speak as though God is real and is with you. Do not empower your doubts by mulling over them, arguing against them, or pursuing them. Do all you can to turn your attention to the truths of God's Word — to the reality of Jesus.

There are no easy answers to the hardness of life. But we can know that Jesus foresaw these attacks, and He has called us to stand in the face of them.

14 DARKNESS, DEMONS, & GLORY

"When Jesus had called the Twelve together, he gave them power and authority to drive out all demons and to cure diseases, and he sent them out to proclaim the kingdom of God and to heal the sick." -- Luke 9:1-2

"Look, I have given you authority over all the power of the enemy, and you can walk among snakes and scorpions and crush them. Nothing will injure you. But don't rejoice because evil spirits obey you; rejoice because your names are registered in heaven." -- Luke 10:19-20 (NLT)

"This is such a dark place."
"You'd better be really prayed up when you go there. There's so much demonic activity."
"You could feel the oppression."

So often when I talk to people who are going on, or have returned from, a short-term mission trip, I hear statements similar to the above. I hear the same thing about certain parts of this nation, or even areas of my city.

When I lived in the town of Masaka, in Uganda, the hardness of the town was one of the favorite topics of conversation among the local pastors. There seemed to be a kind of competition, as each one searched for greater evidence of the unusual darkness that haunted the place of their chosen ministry.

"Man, Evangelist so-and-so came here, and said he'd never come back again. Nobody got saved."

"Did you hear that [insert name of well-known preacher] refuses to come to Masaka? He says people are too hard-hearted here."

"You know that this is one of the centers of witchcraft in Uganda, right? That's why ministries struggle so much."

Why are we so enamored by "darkness?" Is it a kind of pride, that makes us feel like super heroes for going to places we consider hard? I'm really not sure. But, oddly enough, I don't see much of this in scripture. Instead, I see Jesus bringing light everywhere He went. I see the apostles continuing in the same manner after the Resurrection. It is true that in His hometown of Nazareth, Jesus did not heal many people (Mark 6:5). However, that is not associated with the demonic or a plague of "darkness," but rather the people's lack of faith that came from the fact that they had watched Jesus grow up.

When seventy-two of Jesus' followers were sent out to proclaim the kingdom, it was God's glory that they discovered in the hinterlands of Galilee. When they encountered darkness, they were commissioned to overcome it. It was God's power that made a lasting impression on them. (Luke 10:17-24). When God sent Moses into the heart of pagan Egypt, it was the glory of the Almighty that people could not help but notice.

"My great glory will be displayed through Pharaoh and his troops, his chariots, and his charioteers. When my glory is displayed through them, all Egypt will see my glory and know that I am the LORD!" -- Exodus 14:17-18 (NLT)

The enemy is at work throughout the earth. His destruction and desecration are evident. He undoubtedly has more success in some places than in others. But do not be in awe of his power. Compared with the strength of the Almighty whom you serve, it is nothing. There is not one instance when God's people are warned in scripture to be extra careful in a particular place because the oppression is of unusual intensity there. There is always an assumption that when God shows up in His people, it is the enemy that must give way. The people of God are not threatened by the presence of demons; It is the demons who tremble at the mention of Jesus.

In short, be impressed with the glory of God, not the works of darkness. Everywhere. Always.

Open your eyes! His glory is evident in this world. In India, I have stood under a sacred tree in a Hindu city awash with grotesque idols and the worship of countless would-be gods. In Uganda, I have walked through an arid and poverty-stricken refugee camp where tens of thousands lived in terror of a wicked witch doctor named Kony. In Mexico, on the "Day of the Dead" -- a day dedicated to the worship of the spirit of death, whose images filled the city -- I have prayed in a red-light district run by the Mexican drug cartels. In the United States, I have sat with homeless people, strung out on drugs and brimming over with hatred and violence. I've even treaded the halls of shopping malls among hundreds of mammon-worshipers carrying out their fruitless search for meaning and fulfillment. And in each of those places, along with many others, I have seen the glory of God. Please hear me! I have seen His glory. Jesus was there.

In Mexico, I saw Him in the boundless joy of a former prostitute and drug addict whom He had set free. In India, I saw Him in a small group of faithful servants, together standing against the tide of deception and bondage in their country. In Uganda, I experienced Him in the exuberant and defiant worship of Christians who had lost nearly everything gathering together to pray. In Tulsa, I have seen Him in the poor as they show simple kindness and give thanks for small blessings.

Jesus heals the sick in places we consider dark. He casts out demons. He transforms lives. He sets people free. He brings new life.

Do not be afraid! How many times times does Jesus say this to His timid followers? You are secure in His love, and that is what matters. His love is the greatest power in the universe. And it is directed towards you. Man!

"What then shall we say to these things? If God is for us, who is against us? He who did not spare His own Son, but delivered Him over for us all, how will He not also with Him freely give us all things? Who will bring a charge against God's elect? God is the one who justifies; who is the one who condemns? Christ Jesus is He who died, yes, rather who was raised, who is at the right hand of God, who also intercedes for us. Who will separate us from the love of Christ? Will tribulation, or distress, or persecution, or famine, or nakedness, or peril, or sword?

"Just as it is written, 'For your sake we are being put to death all day long; We were considered as sheep to be slaughtered.'

"But in all these things we overwhelmingly conquer through Him who loved us. For I am convinced that neither death, nor life, nor angels, nor principalities, nor things present, nor things to come, nor powers, nor height, nor depth, nor any other created thing, will be able to separate us from the love of God, which is in Christ Jesus our Lord." -- Romans 8:31-39 (NASB)

Please do me a favor, and read that again. And read it any time you are tempted to be impressed by some work of the demonic. Also, remember this: Jesus has given you authority over the enemy and his works, but that gift is a mere trinket as compared with the greatness of His love for you.

"Look, I have given you authority over all the power of the enemy, and you can walk among snakes and scorpions and crush them. Nothing will injure you. But don't rejoice because evil spirits obey you; rejoice because your names are registered in heaven." -- Luke 10:19-20 (NLT)

Every year as I interact with people preparing for mission trips, one of the big concerns is the spiritual warfare or the darkness of where they are going. *Don't be afraid!* You're going to be fine. Jesus loves you.

If we are good on that point, we can now address the issue of destroying the works of the enemy. Sometimes the spirit war, as I wrote in the previous section, is internal and nebulous. The enemy lurks in the murky mists of doubt and fear and depression and failure. But sometimes it is more in-your-face. Standing before you, there is a sick person whom you long to see healed, or a demonized soul that needs to be delivered. Whether you asked for it or not, you are confronted with a power encounter between the forces of darkness and the strength of your God. You feel the eyes of curious onlookers set on you, waiting to see what will happen. Inside, you are a tangle of fear and hope and faith and confusion and pressure and desperation. What do you do?

I would like to make a suggestion for you: Heal the sick. Drive out the demons.

This is your commission. You have the power to do this. Right now. The power that raised Jesus from the dead dwells in you. Right now. You do not need to work anything up. You do not need to go to the spiritual gym. This isn't Rocky. This is the power of God. What, then, is your part? You have to *believe*. Read the Gospels. Read Acts. Faith is the thing that comes up again and again in connection with the miraculous and the powerful. You have to *trust* Jesus. You have to trust Him in that moment when you are praying for the sick. In that moment when you are confronted with the bizarre behavior coming from a demonized soul.

Your power is not in the way you pray. It is not in your volume or your inflection or your eloquence or how authoritative you can make your voice sound. It is in the presence of the Spirit of God who is within you, and it is in you trusting that Spirit. A few other simple thoughts may help as well:

First, work together. It may be that your contacts have a lot of experience in dealing with the demonic or in praying for the sick. Learn how to cooperate with them. Also, work with your teammates. You can encourage one another and challenge one another. While one of you is engaging with the person, others can be quietly praying.

Secondly, listen for the voice of the Spirit. Do not force anything, and do not try to get weird. But listen. He does speak, and He does give you the ability to hear Him. If you have an impression as you pray, step out in obedience, or check with a teammate to get confirmation. Sometimes you may realize that the thing you are praying for actually isn't the biggest need -- so don't be afraid to pray as He leads you.

Thirdly, fight for compassion and love. Sometimes we can get so focused on our desire to see God's power at work that we are no longer motivated by compassion. Look at the person. Ask Jesus to give you His love for him or her. Pray because you want to see Jesus glorified in this person's life, not just because you want to have a great experience of God's power. It's subtle, but significant.

Fourthly, just do it. Seriously. Step out. Take the risk. Do not worry about the outcome. If you begin praying for people, you will encounter failure. You will pray with no apparent result. But don't stop. You certainly will not see people delivered if you do not step out. Do not focus on what doesn't happen. Focus on Jesus. He is with you. He has sent you. He has commissioned you. He has empowered you.

The spirit war is real, but the victory was won at the Cross. Fight. Engage. But don't fear. Don't try too hard. The power is in Jesus. Have faith. And have fun. Discover the glory of Jesus right where you are.

15 TOGETHER

Being part of a team on Jesus' mission is one of the most rewarding and difficult and wonderful experiences you can have. You will accomplish so much more together. You will experience a depth of relationship that may astound you. You will come to love and appreciate these friends. You will be frustrated and annoyed and angry. You will want to get away and you will probably lose your temper. But Jesus is in this. It is His way. Ministry happens together.

We know that Jesus had His twelve and that He sent them out two by two. Paul travelled on a team. David had his mighty men. And God most likely has people that He wants you to partner with for His great cause. These may not always be the ones you would choose, but His choice is better. Always.

So how do we do this well? Yes, it can be a disaster, and maybe you've experienced that. But the potential is so worth every effort. You can reach people with the love of Jesus when you are committed to doing it together in a way you cannot do otherwise.

"Above all, you must live as citizens of heaven, conducting yourselves in a manner worthy of the Good News about Christ. Then, whether I come and see you again or only hear about you, I will know that you are standing together with one spirit and one purpose, fighting together for the faith, which is the Good News." -- Philippians 1:27 (NLT)

"Standing together with one spirit and one purpose, fighting together." Your team relationships matter more than you might think. So take time together. Pray together. Have fun together. Talk together. Share your stories. And your dreams and frustrations; your victories and failures; your hopes and disappointments. It may seem counterintuitive, but the time you put into being friends with your co-laborers is extremely significant. Sometimes eating ice cream together or playing games is the most Kingdom-like thing you can do. A saying in the network of friends of which I am apart is that *the Kingdom of God moves at the speed of relationships.* It is better to accomplish less in the short-term in order to build long-term friendships.

For the past eight years, I have joined together (most) every Thursday evening with a group of friends to provide a meal for the homeless and to welcome them into a family meal. Working closely with the poor can be a draining experience, and we all face times of discouragement and weariness. One of the primary things that has enabled me to continue in this ministry is the friendships that have developed through it. Often I do not want to show up, but the thing that gets me there is knowing my friends will be there. I know they are counting on me, but I also genuinely look forward to seeing them. I can go from complaining about having to be there to actually looking forward to it by simply thinking about my friends. And we have come to realize that we have to cultivate this. There have been times when motivation is more and more difficult to generate. Often what helps is to spend extra time with my team. We'll go out for ice cream afterwards or all get together in one of our homes. We'll laugh together and share frustrations and hopes. As our hearts are knit together more deeply, I experience the joy of "standing together with one spirit and purpose."

Of course, it's often more difficult than I am making it seem. Sometimes your team is just not that awesome. They are mundane and un-special. So disappointing, especially when you consider who could have been part of this with you. Maybe it is even worse than that. Fred is so ridiculously annoying. Freda is bossy. Your leader is pompous. Joe is domineering. Josephine is insecure. One pathologically self-centered. Another is moody. They're all more than a little awkward. It takes all you have just to be civil. Talking about deep friendship with these morons is so not inspiring.

Welcome to the Kingdom of God.

Welcome to the Family.

Here are a few thoughts that might help:

1. You fit in with this crew so much more than you realize because you are one of the morons. Seriously. Your weakness and brokenness are pretty much on the same level as theirs. As much as this may not seem to be good for your self-esteem issues, I want to encourage you to embrace the reality of your own fallenness. When I risk even a shallow peek into my own heart -- when I take note of my words and my behaviors and my attitudes and my thoughts -- I become uncomfortably aware that I am no better than the worst of them. Paul actually advises the Philippians to "think of others as better than yourselves." (2:3). Think on that. Do not rationalize it and say, "well, he doesn't mean..." Just take it at face value and practice it.

2. You fit into this crew so much more than you realize because, not only are you just as much of a moron as them, but even moreso because they are a truly amazing and gifted group of people. I know this because every one of us has been created uniquely by God. He has endowed them with gifts and has filled their hearts with passions. He considers them worth the suffering and death of the cross. And He considers you the same. Be intentionally wowed by these people because God is revealing a part of His nature through them.

3. This is bigger than you. You have to be friends with these people because it is for the Kingdom! It is for the glory of Jesus! It is so worth it. Think of how He condescends to be your friend! Is it because you are so amazing?

"After the Lord your God has driven them out before you, do not say to yourself, 'The Lord has brought me here to take possession of this land because of my righteousness... It is not because of your righteousness or your integrity that you are going in to take possession of their land... Understand, then, that it is not because of your righteousness that the Lord your God is giving you this good land to possess, for you are a stiff-necked people." Deuteronomy 9:4-6

There is a lot at stake here. Your friendships will help to advance the Kingdom. Will set people free. Will demonstrate the goodness and the love of the Father to the world. Will defeat the works of darkness. Will exalt Jesus. You need them in order to do all this. You need them. Do not take them for granted or assume the work you have to do is more important than these relationships.

4. God has chosen these people for you and you for them. Choose to believe this. In our community, we have committed ourselves to believe that every person who comes to us has been sent by Jesus. Every person who comes to my home. Every person who comes to our community meal. Every person who comes to a gathering. It is so easy to dream about the perfect team. It is so easy to be jealous of what others seem to have. But what if these are the people God has given to you? What if the very things that make them difficult are good for your soul? Are making you more like Jesus? I have wished -- and even prayed -- to be free of particular people. But God nearly always ends up convicting me of something in my own heart. He helps me to see the value of the other person and the character that needs to develop in me. There is no utopian ideal. Even your dream team would end up being very difficult, because we are all fallen people still in need of the mercy and grace of Jesus every single day. Accept your team as God's gift.

16 THURSDAY NIGHT LIGHT STORY

In desperation, Jesse uttered what would become a life-changing prayer. "If you're there, God, and you love me, please somehow tell me today. If not, I'm going to kill myself." Life certainly was not what he had planned to this point. Tumultuous teenage years had passed into an even rockier young adulthood. A brief stint in the army didn't help. Alcohol, drugs, and partying didn't seem to be the thing either. He never thought he would sink to the depths of being homeless, sleeping in a car, doing anything to just get by. But he had. In a desperate attempt to get his life back on track, he had taken this job selling magazines door-to-door. A place to stay and a little money was nice. But nothing touched the ache in his soul, and it was hard to convince himself that life was worth living. And then the prayer.

That same fateful day, walking down the street in an unfamiliar city, his heart filled with dark thoughts and suicidal plans, it all changed. A man stepped out of his front door and called out, "Young man, I have something to tell you." Jesse turned, dubious. "God loves you so much, and He wanted me to tell you so."

Stunned. Did that really just happen?

Tears began to flow as Jesse's hardened heart exploded within his chest. The Spirit of God broke in like a flood. And in that moment, Jesse knew it was true. God loved him. Was actually pursuing him. Had heard his pitiful prayer, and was even now responding. It was too much to take in. But this man, this messenger of the Father, was now embracing him, and the weary and restless prodigal was coming home.

I met Jesse a few months later, and we became friends. He had responded to the Father's call, turned his back on the old life, and returned home to his praying mother. Things were not suddenly easy, and the old nature was still fighting for life, but Jesse was a new man. That much was clear. More months passed, and Jesse's transformation continued. There were setbacks and failures, but the life of Jesus, which had so radically invaded his soul, was more and more taking over every part of Jesse's heart. It didn't take long before this new tenderness to God's Spirit began to express itself in a tenderness and love for people -- especially those who were even yet living in the same darkness and despair from which he had so recently been delivered. We spent time praying together about this, and asking the Father how He would work through Jesse to demonstrate His love to others.

It wasn't obvious that God was answering this prayer one day when Jesse and a buddy encountered a homeless man who was asking for money. But He was. Without anything to give to the man, Jesse and his friend had the idea to invite him to a cook-out. They had a habit of hanging out with friends and eating together on Thursday evenings, so why not invite this man? In fact, maybe this homeless man had some friends that he'd also like to invite? Their suggestion was accepted, and it was agreed that they would meet back up in the evening at Owen Park.

Something of the eternal and glorious Kingdom of God was happening that day. In obscure Owen Park, on the edge of downtown Tulsa, a few friends got together and grilled hot dogs, played basketball, and began getting to know each other. About fifteen homeless people came and enjoyed the meal and the friendship. At the end of the evening, after some simple prayers and reluctant good-byes, someone called out to Jesse as he pulled away, "See you next week?" And so it began. That was eight years ago. Every Thursday night a group of friends still gets together, cooks some food, and shares it with whoever will come. We also share the truth of Jesus' love, worship Him together, and sit at tables enjoying food and friendship. It's so simple.

Jesse, along with his friends James and Karissa, pioneered and led this "Owen Park Outreach" for several years. Sometimes they had no money or food on Thursday morning, but they always had a meal for as may as would show up by Thursday night. They persevered through the cold of winter and heat of summer, through bitter disappointments, and too many heartbreaking situations to recount. They became genuine friends with people living on the streets, and helped some to move on to better things. Eventually they attracted like-minded friends to help them, and were able to hand off the meal and planning to others. Now, several local churches and more than a dozen volunteers continue to come together in the same spirit each Thursday night. A welcoming invitation is given. People are loved and accepted. Friendships are made. The Gospel is proclaimed. Prayers are offered. The kingdom is coming.

I've been one of the many who have had the privilege to come along as a helper and a learner, being challenged and equipped by the Holy Spirit through this trio of friends. The following is from my journal -- an entry I stumbled across from March, 2013. It's pretty "typical" in many ways:

The Thursday of Easter Week at Owen Park is always a special evening. It is such a great opportunity to talk to people about the love of Christ, and how He sacrificed Himself for us in order to free us from sin and all its consequences... We gathered in a circle under the pavilion, and James clearly and powerfully gave testimony to the love of Jesus, and invited us to reach out to Him. Just as he was winding up, and beginning to transition into the Communion time, everyone's attention was suddenly diverted to the basketball court.

"He just decked him! I saw it! Just laid him out! I saw it!" a woman standing next to me excitedly repeated multiple times, as everyone swarmed to the court. A man was indeed laying there, surrounded by others enthusiastically sharing what had happened. Eventually he was able to stand, and, other than a nasty knot on his head, seemed to be ok. While some of the crew helped to restore order there, we re-convened in the pavilion. However, I must admit it was a somewhat distracted ring of humanity that I tried to lead into the joyful solemnity of the Lord's Supper. Fortunately, by this time several of our ORU contingent were playing music and singing worship songs. This helped to bring more of an atmosphere of peace. In spite of the excitement, it was a joy to stand there and serve the elements to individuals deeply loved by God, and to pray for them. "The Body of Christ, broken for you. The Blood of Christ, poured out for you."

As the food was being served, and things settled back to "normal," an older man new to the park asked the ORU group if he could try out their guitar. It turned out he was quite a musician, and we all had fun listening and encouraging him as he reveled in the opportunity to shine, and to do something that was clearly a joy to him. In chatting with him briefly later, I learned that his name is David.

As I reflect on the events of this evening, I waver between discouragement, hope, and something else... maybe just amusement. Owen Park. Few of us in this city probably have the opportunity to lead a group of people in the Lord's Supper after the Gospel presentation was broken up by a fight. God, what are you doing? What is this crazy place you have me serving? Why me? Why here? I am pathetic at this. And yet, why do I kind of like it? And why do I really not like it some of the time? And did I mention, why me? Very amusing.

Jesus is at work, pursuing and redeeming lost humanity. He deeply cares about your city and your school. Your workplace, your neighborhood, your family. Your outreach and your normal life. Your church and your favorite hang-out spot. Like Jesse, what He has done for you, He longs to do through you. And, if you are willing, He will. He is able to work beyond your limitations and weaknesses. He really is.

17 TNL LESSONS

In the last section, I told you about the beginning of the outreach we now call Thursday Night Light. In those first years, the small band of young friends -- Jesse, James, and Karissa -- provided all the labor and leadership and finances for the ministry. They were soon joined by Katie and Rachel (now James' and Jesse's wives). This company of Kingdom servants have impacted the lives of many, including middle-class church folk and down-and-out homeless and poor folk. Along the way, they've taught me some essential lessons, three of which I want to share here.

First, *we need each other.* Upon moving to Tulsa in 2007, I began praying for and seeking a significant way to minister to the poor. I had become convinced that this was the Lord's heart for His Church, but I wasn't at all sure how to go about it. I'd had some helpful experiences in Uganda and Detroit, but I had much to learn. This was not necessarily in my mind when I first heard about the dinners happening at Owen Park. In fact, cooking hot dogs for homeless people would not have been a strategy I would have appreciated. However, Jesse was my good friend and I felt it would be right to support him in this endeavor. I didn't know if it would last for a few weeks, or all summer, or beyond. So on the second or third week, I made it out to the park to check things out.

At this point, I have to explain a couple of things about myself. First of all, I am not an outgoing person. I do not particularly like crowds of people, tend to be easily intimidated, and do not do well at making conversation or engaging with new people. I also avoid conflict and begin to feel anxious if I even hear others arguing or raising their voices. So to say that I was out of my comfort zone at Owen Park would be putting it mildly. I clearly remember driving up on that early summer evening. Getting out of my car, I searched for Jesse's familiar face, and spotted it with a sense of relief. Approaching him, I asked what I could do to help. In typical fashion, he suggested that I just chill and talk with folks. Great.

As I continued hanging out on Thursday evenings over the course of the summer, Jesse, James, and Karissa would introduce me to their new friends. Through them, I began to get to know the poor and found that I could have meaningful conversations with them. Sometimes these would be serious, personal, or spiritual. More often they were casual and full of joking and swearing. But I was getting to know people, learning to care for them, pray for them, and share the Gospel. In all of this, Jesse, Karissa, and James were my unwitting mentors. I watched them, joined conversations that they initiated, connected with them in prayer, and got to know their friends. It seemed so easy and natural to them, and so strained and unnatural to me. But I was learning.

At some point early on, it hit me. We're in this together. I am not bestowed with the same gifts as my friends, and vice versa. I could never have initiated a ministry like this in a million years, but I could contribute in meaningful ways and even add something that was lacking. We needed each other. And more.

At the end of that eventful summer, we launched the Tulsa Boiler Room, a "simple church" that would be devoted to prayer, to spiritual family, to the Gospel, and to loving the poor. Over the next couple of years, James, Katie, Karissa, Jesse, and Rachel led the way in inviting the poor and homeless we were meeting on Thursday nights into the experience of Christian family that we were building on Friday and Tuesday nights. And I began to see people getting involved in the lives of the poor without typically going out on Thursdays. They would welcome them into their house church groups, pray with them, help them in practical ways, and show them acceptance and love. In fact, I've become convinced that we cannot make a lasting difference with the poor without the support of such a community. We need to not only go out, but we need to pray. And we need to not only pray, but to invite people in.

Karissa, James, and Jesse could not do this alone. And I could not do it alone. And together, we still needed others. And this is the way of the Kingdom. The Father has willed it to be so.

Friendship is a great start to ministry. The Proclamation of the Gospel is powerful -- perhaps the most powerful tool in our belt. However, an environment of friendship, acceptance, and kindness provides the best opportunity for the Gospel to do its transformational work. God likes it when we make friends with non-Christian people. Even with immoral people. Nasty people. With atheists and pagans and Muslims. Certainly with the poor and the homeless, the addicted and the violent, the lost and confused. Jesus was clearly friends with all kinds of disreputable people, and this is part of our calling.

Shorty is one of my friends. We've known each other for about eight years. I think we were a couple years into our relationship before I ever saw him sober. Shorty has a great personality, is a lot of fun, and can be a big troublemaker. He was consistently getting kicked out of the local shelters because of belligerence and violence. He's a smartelic of the highest order. I've had to break up fights that he was determined to start, talk him down from bursts of anger, and listen to his ravings about what he's going to do to so-and-so. But more than that, I've enjoyed a lot of good times with him. Lots of bad jokes and story-telling. There have been a few times other friends and I have openly shared the Gospel with Shorty, prayed for him, and spoken from the heart. I treasure those moments. We have certainly prayed for him a lot. James and Katie used to get regular calls from him in the night, and they would go out and bring him a sandwich or a blanket to help him make it until morning.

Some time ago, after a long uphill struggle, lots of help from various people and agencies, and the persevering determination of our friend and co-laborer Paul Schmidt, Shorty got an apartment. I'm so excited for him. He volunteers with us at our outreach center for the homeless, showing up for work with a smile each day. I don't know how it's all going to turn out with him, but I do know that I value our years of friendship. I also know that, because of this, he is more apt to listen when I share with him. I so want him to receive the freedom and deliverance and adoption that Jesus is offering. The Gospel is still his only hope. But, for Shorty and many like him, friendship comes first and has a value all its own.

Ministry <u>with</u> is better than ministry <u>at</u>. Karissa tells a classic story from Owen Park like this:

> "One winter night, a young girl came along with her family to help serve the Thursday night meal. Baffled at what she saw, she came to me and said, 'I don't know who the special people are.' Everyone was bundled up against the cold that night. During the winter, it's almost impossible to tell who are those who have come to be served and those who have come to serve. Honestly, the line blurs on that anyway.
>
> "Oftentimes, the people who come to Owen Park to be fed will in turn help cook, serve the food and clean up afterward. We like to empower people that this is not a soup kitchen, this is not a hand-out line, this is a family dinner. That permeates the philosophy of how we do everything, whether it be how we serve food to how we deal with altercations between people to a myriad of things."

I have learned to appreciate those blurry lines more and more. The lines between the 'ministers' and the 'ministered to.' Between the 'needy' and the 'prosperous.' Between the objects of mission and the missionary. I can influence people towards Jesus more effectively when I do it as a friend and a servant more than as an expert and a professional. When people cannot figure out whether I'm one of the leaders or one of the homeless, I feel I'm in a good place. There is great power in identification and in incarnation. This is good for me, because it is a blow to my ever-grasping pride and arrogance. It is good for my friends because it helps them to know I love them. It is powerful in expressing the Gospel because it comes from a fellow-sojourner who has been given a great gift, and who loves to share that with friends.

"Because we loved you so much, we were delighted to share with you not only the gospel of God but our lives as well." -- 1 Thessalonians 2:8

Sometimes, instead of this, I often want to 'minister at' folks. I want to focus on using my gifts and getting that feeling of accomplishment and satisfaction. I want to be needed and for people to depend on me to give them wisdom or a 'word in season.' This is foolish and harmful. Alternatively, when I 'minister with' I highlight what we have in common and I reveal the dignity and worth of my friends. I receive from them as I offer them the Gospel.

18 THE DEAL CHANGER

To be frank, failure has been a big part of my life. It started in my early days of following the Lord. I failed at the very things I was told Christians must do in order to be true believers: pray daily, read the Bible, and tell others about Jesus. I made many commitments. I responded to altar calls. I repented. I determined to try harder. But it did not work. I was horrified to discover, time and time again, that I could not do it. As an older teenager, and eventually as a young adult, I often faced the inner question of whether or not I was truly saved. Whether I was in God's family. I used to imagine a day in the future when I would have my stuff together and would know I was fully "in." You could say my spiritual walk was tumultuous. Passionate? Yes. Consistent? No. Successful? Hardly.

At the age of twenty-three, I set off with my wife to change the world, beginning with the nation of Uganda. At the age of twenty-six, I crept back to the United States with my tail between my legs. Looking back, of course, I know that God used those three difficult years to develop my character and begin to make me into something He could use. But as far as any actual ministry fruit, well... I was pretty creative when it came to writing newsletters. I returned to the US with the conviction that I had failed and with the desperate hope that I wasn't simply a failure. That there was more to me than that. But to be honest, I wasn't sure.

At this time, the Lord, in His mercy, led us to a church where we learned about the grace of Jesus in a way that we had never understood before. I began to see grace as an actual force in my life, working in me a knowledge of the Father's love, helping me to overcome sin, forgiving me every time I screwed up. This was good. Refreshing. So glad I learned that lesson.

A few years later, we were back at it again. Now, with three young children and renewed confidence, we returned to Uganda to give it another shot. This time we were going to plant a church. That would soon lead to multiple churches. That would soon lead to a national movement. That would... Well, my modesty eventually forced me to stop somewhere.

Nine months later we received a visitor from our home town. Ron Meyers had been my Missions professor in seminary and was part of our sending church. It was a big deal for us when he stepped off the plane at the airport in Entebbe on Jill and my eighth wedding anniversary. We showed him what we were doing, took him to our little church meeting in a rundown old house, and had several long talks. All the while, we were desperately hoping that he was impressed. After a couple of days, however, he looked at me and said what I had been dreading to hear, "This just isn't working for you, is it Tim?"

I had known the truth of this somewhere deep inside, but had not yet found the fortitude to admit it to myself. Failure again? Are you serious? But he was right. It wasn't working. Something was wrong. Something must be wrong with me. Fortunately for me, Ron's bluntness was matched by his wisdom, and he began to point me to areas of actual fruitfulness that he had observed, though I had considered those activities peripheral to my primary mission. After a brief time of grief and pain, I heeded Ron's good advice. Years of fruitful service followed. This time, failure finally gave way to fruitfulness.

I could go on. I remember another moment, years later, when living in the States again. I was feeling hurt and overlooked by people whose approval I desperately desired. I felt rejected and misunderstood. To be honest, I was reeling. "Reverse culture shock" was wreaking havoc on my emotions, my identity, my understanding of life. And that's when Kayita died.

Kayita. How do I write about this? Kayita had been my closest friend for the previous five years. He was the pastor of a small congregation in rural Uganda. He was my ministry partner and the person we had left as primary leader of the work we had initiated there. We had spent countless hours together, traveling around the African bush, drinking endless cups of milky sweet tea, having in-depth conversations about education and politics and history and Uganda and America and the Church, and mostly about Jesus. I had been with him in July on a scouting trip to northern Uganda. And now, in October, he was dead. When I got the news in my faraway home in America, I sank even deeper into despair and darkness.

Kayita's death impacted me on multiple levels. The first, of course, was the deep grieving for a friend. The thought of his being gone was pure agony. It also meant that the ministry we had built together would falter and be forever weakened, quite possibly to not survive at all. One evening a day or two after receiving the news, I was in my house alone, angry and sad and confused. I was still bitter about the rejection I had felt from people and was complaining to the Lord about this. In a moment, I was reminded of a recent email interaction with Kayita, just a couple of months before he passed away -- and it hit me like a load of bricks that I had responded to him in the exact way the people I was complaining about had responded to me. How I must have hurt him! And now he was gone and nothing I could do would make it right. I was devastated. I was angry -- but now, at me. In fact, I was furious. Screaming, sobbing, out of control, I crumpled to the floor.

"You are forgiven." In that moment I knew the Father forgave me. I knew it like I had never known it before. His presence in the room was real and overwhelming, and it was permeated with grace and love. And it was not fair. I should be punished. I should suffer for my insensitivity and my self-centeredness. But, no. Jesus did that for me. For the first time, the grace of God became scandalous. It wasn't right. I continued to weep. It wasn't right. That I should be so thoroughly forgiven. That I should be free from this guilt. At first, this made me even more angry. I wanted to pay for my sin.

But I couldn't. I had nothing to offer to make it right. I was broken, but the Father was making me whole. And that's when I began to see it. The Grace of Jesus is more powerful and more wonderful and more outrageous than I had ever suspected. That night an unexpected sensation began to take hold of me: Joy. I was gripped by wonder; overflowing with gratitude. Failure gave way to an experience of the tenacious, wild, extravagant love of God.

I could go on. I've failed at ministry. I've failed at relationships. I've failed at righteousness. I've failed many times as a father and a husband, as a friend and a pastor. I've let people down. I've judged when I should have forgiven.

Demanded when I should have served. And God loves me. He's not disappointed in me. He's not exasperated. He loves me.

What's the point of this litany of mess-ups? I want you to know this grace because it changes everything. It really does. It changes everything because you too are free to blow it. Maybe everything you've read in this book so far has added to your already unbearable burden. Maybe you have failed with the cultural sensitivity thing. You've failed in prayer. In Bible study. In proclaiming the Gospel. In loving your team. You're still dominated by fear. You just cannot seem to get it right. Praise. the. Lord. Receive His grace. Your failure will give way to fruitfulness. Once it brings you to Jesus as a beggar, finally truly aware that you have nothing to offer Him, nothing to barter with, His power will begin to perfect you.

This grace is a deal changer because once you have experienced it for yourself, you can offer it to others. And it is powerful. Believe me. You do not know what you are carrying. Now you can accept without judging because you yourself have not been condemned! You can speak with confident passion about the scandalous love of God because it has set you free. You can have hope for the lowest of sinners, for the most broken of men, for the most desperate of addicts. Because you have learned that God's power to redeem is far more potent than your power to sin. You can take risks and you can fail repeatedly without stopping because you have become convinced that God's power to lift is greater by far than your ability to screw up. Man, this is good news!

Grace is the deal-changer. Put aside your striving, and for God's sake (literally) stop trying to look perfect. Apart from Christ you can do nothing. But His grace really is amazing. It will change everything if you embrace it.

19 THE PRIZE

"Pray for me? No, God doesn't care about us." I looked past the middle-aged Ugandan man to the small hut in which he lived with his family. And then at the other huts all grouped together, just a few feet apart. Hundreds of them. Thousands, actually. An "Internally Displaced Persons" (IDP) camp in northern Uganda. For 20 years they had lived like this. Not starving to death, thanks to the good will of others, but never satisfied. No hope of leaving or of anything better. Poverty. Dirt. Sickness. Crowds of people. Death. And fear covering all like a blanket.

I had just asked this man, naively it seemed now, if we could pray for him. His simple and despair-filled answer knocked the wind out of me and I had nothing to say. What could I say? In a few days I would be back with my family in our home, far away from this dreadful place. What did I know of his suffering? What kind of comfort or hope or answer did I really think I could offer?

Fortunately, I wasn't alone that day. My friend Kasozi, a pastor from southern Uganda, was there. And he gently but confidently shared the Gospel with this man. He shared about the love of Jesus that is true and eternal no matter what may happen in life. He spoke of the God whose power can transform people from the inside-out. He even dared to speak of hope.

I do not know the rest of this man's story. I never saw him again. But I do know a couple of things. Later that day, I met with others who were in the same situation as he. Living in the same camp. The same conditions. The same lack. And yet they were singing and praising God with exuberant joy. They had discovered something in Jesus that brought them peace in the midst of this awful, chaotic, horror. Truly a peace "beyond understanding," as Paul had claimed.

I also know that later that night, in my room, I repented. I asked Jesus to help me to never again doubt His power. To never lack the courage to speak the Gospel. To never again believe the lie that I have encountered a person for whom Jesus is irrelevant or insufficient. He convicted me to the core of my being with the truth that Jesus Himself is the prize. There are billions of people alive right now who have problems that I cannot hope to understand, let alone solve. Refugees fleeing war and death in the Middle East. Women being exploited in Mexico. Men and women living on the streets in every American city. I do not have the answers. But for each person living in these realities, Jesus is still the great prize, and I can help to lead them to Him.

"The Kingdom of Heaven is like a treasure that a man discovered hidden in a field. In his excitement, he hid it again and sold everything he owned to get enough money to buy the field. Again, the Kingdom of Heaven is like a merchant on the lookout for choice pearls. When he discovered a pearl of great value, he sold everything he owned and bought it!" Matthew 13:44-46

The Kingdom of Heaven is the rule of Jesus. It is the presence of Jesus Himself. Those who are in the Kingdom are those who have put themselves under His rule. They are those who know Christ and trust in Him. To be in the Kingdom is far and away the best thing that could ever be. Nothing comes close to comparing with it. In fact, it would be worth it to give up absolutely everything else to be in the Kingdom. Reputation. Money. Possessions. Family. Friends. Safety. Job. Home. Health. Even life itself. If we gave up all of that, along with anything else we value, it would not even come close to having any significance as compared with the Kingdom, as compared with being in Christ. Jesus made this point over and over in the Gospels.

If this is true — and if we believe the Gospel at all, we have to confess that it is — then what does that say about "ministry" to people? What does it say about love? What thing of value do I truly have to offer any other human being?

I can offer many things. I can offer money, to the extent that I have it. I can give my time. I can use my knowledge or my skills for the sake of others, to help them have a better life. I can offer friendship. Those are good. But, what if I could offer the most ultimate prize in the whole world? What if I could offer the Kingdom? What if I could offer Jesus?

What about those who are less fortunate than me as far as worldly goods and position go? The poor. Refugees. Orphans. The addicted. The imprisoned. The homeless. What do I have for them?

Maybe another way of looking at it would be this: What is the biggest tragedy in a person's life? Is it that they are unemployed? That they have enemies? That they are homeless or in prison or on drugs or in a refugee camp? Is it that people are trying to kill them? Those are all hugely tragic situations, and, as a follower of Jesus, I should do whatever I can to help overcome them. Without a doubt.

But I submit that there is a deeper, darker, and more sinister tragedy by far.

"And what do you benefit if you gain the whole world but are yourself lost or destroyed?" Luke 9:25.

Is it possible that we could help someone overcome drugs, get off the streets, get a job, and have friends, but that they still ultimately be lost or destroyed? That we could in fact help them to 'gain the whole world,' and still they lose everything?

Or, looking at it from another side, is it possible to help people overcome the deepest tragedy of their existence (their separation from the Father) and yet much of their lives still be extremely hard? Is it possible for us to help someone discover the greatest prize in the universe, and yet he still be materially poor?

There was a time someone wanted to follow Jesus, and Jesus responded by saying, "Foxes have dens to live in, and birds have nests, but the Son of Man has no place even to lay his head." (Luke 9:58). If you want to follow me, Jesus told this hopeful seeker, you'll have to be homeless — at least for this next season. But it's worth it.

Don't worry. I am not advocating that we stop trying to help people get housing or jobs or stability in their lives. That we not seek solutions for refugees or rescue for the enslaved. Not at all. In fact, I'd love for us to do more. We have to do more. It is good and right for us to labor in this. It is the heart of our Father.

But in those discouraging moments when we all ask ourselves, "what are we doing?" there is a more significant answer. We are pointing people to the entrance to the Kingdom. We are showing them the field in which the greatest treasure in the universe is buried. We are guiding them to Jesus Himself. At least, I hope that's what we're doing.

Over the past years, I've seen a number of people get off the streets into housing. And I rejoice every time. It is amazing and worth celebrating. And yet, my heart still breaks for some of them, because they have not discovered the treasure. They have what they thought was the greatest thing they needed. A home. In some cases freedom from addictions. In some cases a job. They will often readily acknowledge that God helped them get what they have. But still many have not found the pearl of such value that they would lay down all that they have gained in order to attain it. And so, sadly, as Jesus warned, they are still on the wide path that leads to destruction. And my heart breaks. Some of these I have known well. We've shared many meals together. They have been in my home. We've talked about Jesus and His Kingdom.

There are others — and my heart hurts for them as well — who are still living on the streets or in poverty, but they are living in the Kingdom right where they are. Do I want them to get a better situation? Yes, I do, with all my heart. But I also rejoice for them, because they have found what is the most important.

Sometimes we are tempted to let Jesus be the means to what we consider a greater end. We want people to encounter Jesus so that Jesus will fix their lives. Sober them up. Get them off the streets. Jesus will not be used like that. He is after far more. He is the means, for sure. But He is also the great end. The purpose. The prize. The goal. The only One worth losing everything else for.

I often ask myself, or am asked by others, "What are we doing on Thursday nights?" I still maintain that what we are doing is hugely important. It is not about the food, really. It never has been. It is about us building relationships with the poor and the homeless and the outcast. But it's not ultimately about that either. It is that through the relationships we build we can actually lead our friends into the relationship that will change everything. The relationship with Jesus.

The prize is Jesus Himself. And He has given us the power and the ability to bring Him to others.

"For God was in Christ, reconciling the world to himself, no longer counting people's sins against them. And he gave us this wonderful message of reconciliation. So we are Christ's ambassadors; God is making his appeal through us. We speak for Christ when we plead, 'Come back to God!'" 2 Corinthians 5:19-20

This is amazing. It's what it's all about.

Jesus is the prize. Our friends can know God. And we can help them. Sometimes — many times, I hope, by the grace of God we can help them get off the streets. Sometimes that won't happen, or it won't happen quickly. But even so, our friends can know God.

20 KNOWING JESUS

After spending a full night in prayer, Jesus chose twelve men from among His followers and designated them as His apostles. His purpose for these twelve was clear:

> "Jesus went up on a mountainside and called to him those he wanted, and they came to him. He appointed twelve that they might be with him and that he might send them out to preach and to have authority to drive out demons."
> -- Mark 3:13-15

The first purpose was that 'they might be with Him.' What a statement! As the Gospel stories unfold, we see that Jesus handpicked men to spend lots and lots of time with Him. He invited them into His life in profound ways. By the time He went to the Cross, these men had been given every opportunity to know Jesus intimately and thoroughly. They knew Him in all His moods. In the midst of stress and in quiet, peaceful evenings. They knew Him in His anger and in His tenderness. Each of them experienced -- not just knew about, but experienced -- His forgiveness and grace and mercy. They were privy to His public ministry and His private conversations. They walked with Him in the miraculous and the mundane. They smiled by His side in the midst of public acclaim and adoration, and trembled as He endured frenzied hatred and false accusations. They prayed with Him and ate with Him and walked with Him and laughed with Him.

And this was the plan. This was His great desire. Years later, Paul was filled with longing for this kind of relationship with Jesus:

"I want to know Christ—yes, to know the power of his resurrection and participation in his sufferings, becoming like him in his death..." -- Philippians 3:10

"I keep asking that the God of our Lord Jesus Christ, the glorious Father, may give you the Spirit of wisdom and revelation, so that you may know him better." -- Ephesians 1:17

Because Jesus ascended to Heaven and sent the Holy Spirit, this amazing relationship is no longer limited to a few specially called ones. No. It is abundantly available to you and me, and it is God's desire that we walk in it.

Today, this is the Father's will for you. This is your calling: To know God.

All other aspirations and hopes and ambitions must bow to this. It is the great priority of your life. It must shape your decisions and mold your character. This is your highest calling and your purest pursuit. It is the most generous invitation you will ever receive, and the most significant command for which you will ever be accountable. Next to this, your financial security, your physical health, the joy of family -- all pale in comparison. The acclaim of people, the comforts of life, vocational success -- faint and fleeting shadows. To know God! This is the great end to which we strain with all our energy and passion.

But what does it mean to know God? There is an ambiguity and a vagueness in the way we use that phrase. How do we know Him? What is it like to know Him?

First, a couple of key foundational thoughts:
1   God wants to be known. To be known by you. He is not playing a cruel game of hide and seek in which you can never discover Him. All of scripture points us to a God who wants to be known. It is the very reason we have been given the Bible.

2   Jesus is the great Revelation of God. To know God, we must know Jesus.
    "No one has ever seen God, but the one and only Son, who is himself God and is in closest relationship with the Father, has made him known." -- John 1:18

    "The Son is the image of the invisible God, the firstborn over all creation.... For God was pleased to have all his fullness dwell in him," -- Colossians 1:15, 19

    "For in Christ all the fullness of the Deity lives in bodily form," -- Colossians 2:9

So, how do we know Jesus? What does that mean to you and me today?
    Certainly, there is an intimacy. An *experienced* relationship. An enjoyment of His presence. Repeated encounters with Him. There is emotion and there is affection and there is peace. There is an experience of His love:

"And may you have the power to understand, as all God's people should, how wide, how long, how high, and how deep his love is. May you *experience* the love of Christ, though it is too great to understand fully. Then you will be made complete with all the fullness of life and power that comes from God." -- Ephesians 3:18-19. (NLT. Emphasis added).

We experience Him in different ways. Sometimes it is dramatic. Often it can be more subtle. It happens in corporate worship and in moments of quiet prayer. In reading His Word and participating in the Lord's Supper. It happens through suffering. Through His people assembled together and in private conversations with brothers and sisters in Christ. In serving the poor and proclaiming Him to the lost. In meditation.

We also need to realize that there are different kinds of experiencing Him. We experience Him with our emotions, but also with our intellect and in our relationships. Experiencing Him is key. But it is not all.

An essential part of knowing Jesus is knowing His character -- the very character of God. Understanding what He is like. Knowing what pleases Him and what angers Him or grieves Him. In fact, one of the reasons Jesus came and lived among us was to reveal the Father; to help us to know what He is like.

Many of us enjoy the emotional experiences with Him, but fail to comprehend what He is truly like or who He truly is. This was the case for the majority who followed Him during His earthly ministry and it is still the same today. The crowds sought Him and hung around Him for various reasons, but many -- most -- never truly apprehended Who He was. They experienced Him without knowing Him -- and they were perfectly satisfied with that. Many today are content with the same arrangement. But Jesus Himself is not. Because we are sketchy as to the details of Jesus' character, many of us simply fill in the gaps with our own assumptions or convictions. Thus, we re-create Jesus in our own images, assuming He must correspond with our ideal. Brennan Manning suggests that "There is a tendency in every Christian mind to remake the Man of Galilee, to concoct the kind of Jesus we can live with, to project a Christ who confirms our preferences and prejudices."[13]

As obvious as it seems, we need to remember that Jesus is who He is, not who we wish or assume Him to be. In order to know Him, we must study Him. Listen to Him through the scriptures. Observe His actions and hear His words. Listen as those who were close to Him describe Him. Pay attention as they tell us clearly about the things that please Him.

"We continually ask God to fill you with the knowledge of his will through all the wisdom and understanding that the Spirit gives, so that you may live a life worthy of the Lord and please him in every way: bearing fruit in every good work, growing in the knowledge of God.." Colossians 1.9-10 (NLT).

"Carefully determine what pleases the Lord." -- Ephesians 5:10 (NLT)

Finally, knowing Jesus also implies becoming more like Him.
"But that isn't what you learned about Christ. Since you have heard about Jesus and have learned the truth that

---

[13] Brennan Manning, *The Signature of Jesus* (Colorado Springs: Multnomah Books, 1996), p 151.

117

comes from him, throw off your old sinful nature and your former way of life, which is corrupted by lust and deception." -- Ephesians 4:20-22 (NLT)

"Not everyone who says to me, 'Lord, Lord,' will enter the kingdom of heaven, but only the one who does the will of my Father who is in heaven. Many will say to me on that day, 'Lord, Lord, did we not prophesy in your name and in your name drive out demons and in your name perform many miracles?' Then I will tell them plainly, 'I never knew you. Away from me, you evildoers!'" -- Matthew 7:21-23

"Imitate God, therefore, in everything you do, because you are his dear children." -- Ephesians 5:1 (NLT)

Becoming like Jesus is a cooperative work between you and the Holy Spirit. You cannot truly know Jesus without gradually becoming more and more like Him. If you are not making that effort, you are not walking with Him closely as He desires. You are not living into the full potential of who He created you to be, or accomplishing the good works He prepared for you to do.

There is no intimacy apart from transformation.

There is no true knowledge of God apart from being conformed to His image.

Knowing Jesus is at the very center of your calling. Today He does not limit Himself to twelve people, but invites each of us into a deep and personal relationship. He has selected you to be with Him. Everything else must come after that and out of that.

You are invited and called to know God. But there's more...

21 AND MAKING HIM KNOWN

"Jesus went up on a mountainside and called to him those he wanted, and they came to him. He appointed twelve that they might be with him and that he might send them out to preach and to have authority to drive out demons."
-- Mark 3:13-15

As we said before, your foundational calling is to know God -- to experience Him, know His character, and be conformed to His likeness. But your calling only begins there. There is one other essential element to this, the most important thing about your life. You are to be about His work. He called those original twelve not only to be with Him, but also "that he might send them out to preach and to have authority to drive out demons."

Knowing Jesus cannot be separated from doing His work. He has called you to proclaim to the world the good news that God has come and can be known. That He offers forgiveness and adoption and eternal life. This is the great, all-encompassing mission of God, and you are called to be part of it. As a follower of Jesus, this becomes the great, all-encompassing mission of your life as well. He has commanded you to proclaim the Gospel. He has empowered you to drive out demons. He has ordered you to care for the poor. He has given you His Spirit so that you will be a witness for Him.

We know that Jesus commanded His first apostles to "make disciples of all nations," (Matthew 28:20) and to "proclaim the gospel to all creation" (Mark 16:15). This is our heritage and our calling, too. We have inherited this task for our generation. This is not only the work of the professional minister or the heroic missionary. This is for all of Jesus' followers. This is for you. Your purpose is to make Him known. To proclaim Him. To overcome the works of darkness. To bring redemption.

People in the world are lost. You have to get this. They may have it together on the outside and they may be genuinely happy, and even "good," after a fashion. But they are desperately and utterly lost, and they are headed for judgment and Hell. This is the warning of scripture. This is the reality of the world. Jesus sends us out to rescue those He loves. His great mission is your great destiny. His desire is your calling. He gave His life for this, and He expects you to give yours for the same purpose. This is a bigger deal than your vocation or your family or your finances or your comfort or your safety. It's bigger than your grandest ambitions and your most outlandish dreams.

Jesus is not your highest priority among others. He is your life. Everything else flows out of your calling to know Him and make Him known. Do not try to fit Him in. It is not simply about finding time for Him and His demands. Acknowledge that everything is about Him. Your work days and your weekends. Your family and your friends. Your hobbies and leisure and vacations and ministry and rest and vocation and dreams and... You get the idea. If something in your life is outside of the great end of knowing Him and making Him known, how can you make it so? If you cannot, then prune it off.

All of this should lead to some pretty serious reflection. Are you living as if this is the highest purpose of your existence? How might you need to reorder your life to align with your calling? Maybe this means you devote yourself to a body of believers -- a local church -- not for what services they can render for you, but because these are the people God is calling you to walk alongside in knowing Jesus and making Him known? Maybe you need to reconsider your address? Your vocational priorities? I do not mean to quit your job and become a "full-time minister," but to reconsider why you are in your job or profession to begin with. How might your vocation feed your primary mission? Maybe you do need to make a change. What about your family? They are not simply another burden or a competing priority. How are you being called to lead your family into God's purposes together? What about your money? (Yep, we might as well go there too.) Are you putting too much emphasis on this part of your life? Trusting too much in your financial plan to provide security and comfort, rather than "seeking first the Kingdom of God?"

Please understand, it is not that God does not care about your family or your vocation or your money or your time or your relationships. But if you want fruitfulness in life, if you want to find the sweet spot, you have to lay all of these things down before Him. Please, please hear me. I am not talking about being a super Christian or a higher tier disciple. I'm not talking about getting into the more inner circle of God's Kingdom. This is simply following Jesus, and it is for every one of us who believes in Him. But there is a great promise, too. When you lay all of this down and offer it for the Master to use as He will, to fulfill His purposes, you will find life. You will get what you were searching for all along, but maybe didn't even realize you were.

Then he said to them all: "Whoever wants to be my disciple must deny themselves and take up their cross daily and follow me. For whoever wants to save their life will lose it, but whoever loses their life for me will save it." -- Luke 9:23-24

Jesus has work for you! It is a wonderful work, and the most meaningful you could ever do. He has called you to be with Him and to know Him and to carry His redemptive message to the world. Do not miss out on this for lesser goals.

Maybe the Spirit of God has stirred you already and you want to respond, but genuinely do not know how. The two suggestions I have for you are pretty simple, but important. The first is simply to pray. Pray daily, asking Jesus to show you His work for you. Ask Him to connect you with others with whom you can fulfill the part that He has planned for you. And the second is to actively seek out a church body that will welcome you and demand of you and equip you and send you. Then commit to that church through thick and thin. You will accomplish far more with them than you ever could alone.

Jesus loves you deeply and profoundly. He loves you more than you can imagine. And in this love, He is calling you to be with Him and to work with Him. It will impact everything and it will be hard. But it is worth it. Because He is worth it.

22   ALL FOR JESUS

Sometimes I get overwhelmed with the darkness and evil and suffering that are in the world, and I wonder if I can really make any difference. I am so small, and the world can be SO dark! I see street children in Africa with none to love them or tell them that they are valuable. Girls and boys caught in the dark evil of human trafficking. Refugees having lost everything, fleeing violence, fear, and death with nobody to take them in. Homeless men and women in my own city, trapped in cycles of addiction and poverty and the never-ending drama of the streets. Is it worth it to throw myself into trying to bring God's light and love? Well, of course I'm going to say it is. And it is... Yet sometimes hope is hard to find.

I see a raging enemy in a land that I love -- the enemy of our souls. However, with eyes fixed on Jesus in genuine worship, I am given a different perspective. I begin to see that the nations have a Lover and a Lord that is more determined and more persistent and more passionate and more powerful than their dreaded enemy. Jesus really does care about every tear that is cried, every prayer that is prayed, every despairing wail. In fact, I am sure I would never care one little bit if it wasn't for Him giving me the care and the burden. He does have a plan and a purpose, and He will bring it about... somehow.

A mighty fortress is our God, a bulwark never failing;
Our helper He, amid the flood of mortal ills prevailing:
For still our ancient foe doth seek to work us woe;
His craft and power are great, and, armed with cruel hate,
On earth is not his equal.

Did we in our own strength confide, our striving would be losing;
Were not the right Man on our side, the Man of God's own choosing:
Dost ask who that may be? Christ Jesus, it is He;
Lord Sabaoth, His Name, from age to age the same,
And He must win the battle.

And though this world, with devils filled, should threaten to undo us,
We will not fear, for God hath willed His truth to triumph through us:
The Prince of Darkness grim, we tremble not for him;
His rage we can endure, for lo, his doom is sure,
One little word shall fell him.

That word above all earthly powers, no thanks to them, abideth;
The Spirit and the gifts are ours through Him Who with us sideth:
Let goods and kindred go, this mortal life also;
The body they may kill: God's truth abideth still,
His kingdom is forever.[14]

---

[14] "A Mighty Fortress is Our God" by Martin Luther

In *Character of the Lord's Worker*, Watchman Nee talks about having a 'mind to suffer.' It goes something like this: God fully loves blessing us, filling our lives with good things, and all that. He is a loving Father. This is so obvious when you read the Bible. But if I really want to make my life useful to Him and His Kingdom -- to be a true witness that brings others to Jesus, to bring Him glory here and now, to set people free who are suffering and bound by darkness -- then I need to make some choices. I have to be willing to choose to forgo some of the good stuff. Maybe a lot of it. I have to have a mind to suffer; a willingness to accept any difficulty, discomfort, pain, loss, danger, or even death in order to fulfill His work. This is also obvious when you read the Bible -- and history. How much do I really love Jesus? How much do I truly care about the passion of His heart (bringing redemption to the world)? How far am I willing to go with this?[15]

Before I proposed to Jill, I had to buy a ring. I had no money. So that memorable summer I worked my little hiney off. It was not fun work. It was physically hard. It was hot. It was lonely. Nobody around. I did not reward myself by spending the money on stuff I wanted. I lived very simply. But all the while it was so sweet. While I worked and sweated, I thought about Jill. I planned out the engagement event. I composed a poem to her. I lived that blessed moment over and over a thousand times before it ever occurred. I filled my imagination with thoughts of life with her. It was beautiful. What a great summer. I did not like the work, but nor did I complain. I longed for the time of actual reward, but just the expectation of it was enough to make life good.

---

[15] Watchman Nee, *Character of the Lord's Worker* (Anaheim: Living Stream Ministry, 1996).

I now have a beautiful eternity to look forward to, and a wedding party to yearn for. Whatever I sacrifice or suffer for Jesus now will only make that all the sweeter. So Lord, put me to work in any way you will. I am ready.

I am so hungry for my life to count for Jesus. It is awesome that He has called me to be with Him. It is beyond amazing. He likes me! He wants to hang with me... not just in a prayer closet, but all the time -- at basketball games and at home and definitely at my favorite coffee shop. But He also wants to let me work with Him in the things that are closest to His heart -- saving the lost, making disciples, changing the world. This is what I am deciding: If Jesus really is inviting me to be part of this, I want to give it my all. I do not want to hold back or to be weighted down by the need for comfort or by my own desires or by sin or by preferences or anything. He is so incredible, and I want to go all the way for Him. Some people say we should live to get all we can out of life. I want to lose my life in the pursuit of Jesus and His plans and dreams.

A movie called "The Last Samurai" illustrates this well, portraying a picture of complete abandonment and passion. In the movie, an attempt is made to kill the samurai. In trying to ascertain who was behind the murderous scheme, one person suggested that perhaps it was the emperor who was trying to kill him. The samurai's response was, "If the emperor wants me dead, all he has to do is ask." What if our Lord demanded our life? Jesus did say something about "take up your cross daily." I spend a lot of time and effort and even energy in prayer trying to attain the good life. I want personal fulfillment. Happiness. Pleasure. Comfort. Blah, blah, blah. But I want to jump into loving and serving Jesus with full abandonment. Beginning now.

23   PASSIONS[16]

When I graduated from college, my ambitions were simple. I wanted to change the world. I was idealistic and maybe more than a little foolish. My heart had been set ablaze by the fire of Jesus' love, and my imagination captured by His mission to bring redemption to all of creation. I was gripped by the conviction that this was worth living and dying for. I was convinced that we could make a difference. That people's lives could be transformed and their very souls rescued. That families and communities and even nations could be changed. As I said, idealistic and youthful. Probably immature. Unrealistic.

More than a quarter of a century has passed, and I can't seem to grow up.

I still am enraptured by the vision of changing the world. Every time I read "Go and make disciples of all nations," something inside me leaps. Or, "What good would it do you to gain the whole world but lose your soul?" Or, "Proclaim the gospel to every creature." My heart has been irrevocably infected. I cannot shake it.

So I'm just gonna run with it.

---

[16] Floyd McClung, *You See Bones, I See an Army* (Seattle: YWAM Publishing, 2007), pgs 191-205.

Looking back over the past twenty-five years, I do not wish I had taken fewer risks, or made more money, or been more stable. I do not regret moving across the world or raising my kids in Africa or planting a church in Tulsa. I'm not sorry that I seem to have missed the American Dream of ever-increasing prosperity, security, comfort, and status. I certainly do not regret that I have more friends who live under bridges than in mansions. In fact, I have intentionally chosen the things about which I want to be passionate.

Our passions are the things we are willing to suffer for; perhaps even die for. They are what we would sacrifice all else to pursue and attain. They are what drive our decisions, and they are reflected in our calendars and our bank accounts. You can choose them. In fact, you must. If you do not intentionally choose your passions, an ungodly culture, or "corrupt generation," (Acts 2:40) will do so for you.

The foundational passion of any follower of Jesus must be to love Him and make Him known. This is basic to being a Christian. All else must flow from that. *All* else. From there, I have developed four personal passions that I endeavor to keep at the core of what my life is all about. These are:

1   To be a godly husband and father -- to love and care for my family.
2   To reach the marginalized -- the forgotten, oppressed, and discarded -- with the love of Jesus.
3   To pursue, demonstrate, and teach the reality of the local church as family of God.
4   To raise up, equip, and send out servants who will make disciples of the nations.

The American culture in which I live my life is governed by a set of assumptions. These assumptions are that certain things are to be highly valued and sought, that our passions should conform to the worldly wisdom of the age. I have learned that, without a diligent and persistent fight, the world will win. In me. I will lose the passions I have chosen, and will live out of those my culture insists are better. More sensible. More elegant. More sophisticated. More right.

I could list a good number of these American cultural passions, but I'll just go with a few:

1   Money.

2   Comfort / security.

3   Entertainment / pleasure.

4   Success.

5   Tolerance.

These are the gods of our land, the idols of our worship. And, as such, I hate them.

I will offer this brief word of explanation for the sake of those who are horrified by the idea of me hating money or tolerance or whatever. I hate them as gods that actively compete for my worship and seduce those I love. I hate them as idols that are set up as the things we should consider ultimate. I hate the insidious way the world around me pulls me to value them. I still use money. I have a favorite sports team. I love hot showers. But I am wary. Fair enough?

My heartfelt prayer for you is that you will stay close to Jesus and represent Him well. This is my prayer for my children and for all whom I love. Not that they will be wealthy or even comfortable. But that they would know Him! Not that they would be considered nice people who have no enemies, but that they would stand firm in the truth. Not that they would find happiness but that they would be faithful. I confess I do pray for their safety, but never at the expense of obedience or love.

Stay close to Jesus. Represent Him well.

You must intentionally choose your passions and stubbornly hold fast to them. Search the scriptures and find what pleases God. What were the passions of Jesus? Of His apostles?

Write them down. Consult them in every decision. Stay true to them through every test. When financial stress comes, be absolutely determined to still live out of your chosen passions. When relational anxiety overwhelms you, do not stray from the course. When the discouragement of failure or lack or loneliness or ongoing difficulty or insecurity plagues you, please stand firm.

It will really, really help to join yourself to others with like passions. Not necessarily exactly the same, but ones born out of loving Jesus and making Him known. With people who will hold you to your professed values and ideals. Do not be satisfied with a few random people, but make yourself a submitted part of a local church body -- a true spiritual family that is committed to you and can hold you accountable.

It will also help to continually be on your guard. Recognize the various values that are pulling at you. Learn to understand why you want to make certain decisions, and flee from ones made out of the false passions of the world.

You can determine your passions. Choose wisely.

24 ENCOUNTER & ENGAGE

The Bible records some crazy dramatic encounters between people and God. Think about it!

Adam and Eve met with Him in the garden of paradise in the cool of the day. He breathed life into them and provided for them.

Abraham heard Him call from the land of Ur. Later, on a star-speckled night in the desert, he would see the Almighty as a "smoking firepot with a flaming torch (Genesis 15:17). He would hear the promise of descendants like the stars and the sand and of a great nation with mighty kings.

Moses, forty years into a life of exile in the wilderness, met God in a burning bush. The God of Abraham revealed His Name to Moses as YAHWEH, the great I AM.

The people of Israel experienced Him as a pillar of cloud and fire, guiding them through the treacherous wilderness. They felt the ground tremble in His presence at Sinai and saw His fire on the mountain.

Samuel heard His call, waking him three times from sleep.

David met with God as he tended his father's sheep, playing music as an offering of praise. Later, through the prophet Samuel, he was promised a kingdom.

Solomon saw God's glory fill the temple, such that the priests could not enter to perform their duties (2 Chronicles 5:14).

The ancient prophets heard His voice, were granted visions, and were shown His glory. Elijah heard His still small voice. Isaiah trembled before Him in the heavenly court. Ezekiel saw Him as a wheel within a wheel. Daniel met Him in the land of exile.

The twelve disciples met with Jesus on the mountain and were invited to hang out with Him for three years.

On the day of Pentecost, perhaps the greatest encounter so far, the people heard Him coming as a mighty rushing wind and saw the tongues of fire. They received His Spirit to live within them and they spoke in other languages.

Paul met Him on the road to Damascus and was blinded by the light of His brilliance.

God reveals Himself to His people! The awareness -- the feeling -- of the presence of God is a beautiful part of our faith. He invites us into an experiential relationship. He speaks to us. He touches us. He still invades space and time and makes His presence known among us. It happens as we pray and as we worship, as we gather together and as we kneel in our closets. He meets us as we study the scriptures and as we gather with our friends. He invites us to know Him.

The gift of encountering God is wonderful and beautiful. I am so grateful for it.

And yet, something in me is troubled as I consider this reality. Have we cheapened it? In our great desire for the feeling of His presence, have we tried to manufacture it? Do we manipulate through our music and our created atmospheres and ambiance? Something happened to the people in scripture who encountered God. Their lives were marked. They were transformed. And they were given a mission. Every time. Let's go back over our list:

Adam and Eve were told to be fruitful and to fill the earth, to subdue and to rule. Created in the very image of God, they were called to be His representatives. (Genesis 1:28).

Abraham was called to go to a new place, where the LORD would bless him so that he would be a blessing to the nations of the earth. (Genesis 12:1-3).

Moses, of course, was called to lead the people of God out of the slavery of Egypt (Exodus 3:10). The people of Israel themselves were told to possess the Promised Land, that through them the glory of God might be seen by the peoples of the earth. (Deuteronomy 4:1-8).

Samuel was given the task of leading God's people, of restoring the purity of the priesthood, and eventually of anointing the first kings (1 Samuel). David was called to bring revival to his people and to overcome the enemies of God that had oppressed His people for centuries. Solomon was to make the glory of God known among the nations through the ministry in the temple (2 Chronicles 6:33). Elijah was called to confront the prophets of Baal and to train up a new generation of prophets (1 Kings 18-19). Isaiah, Ezekiel, Daniel, and all of the prophets were given specific messages of warning and hope for God's fickle worshipers.

The twelve disciples were called by Him, not only to hang out with Him, but also to go preach and drive out demons (Mark 3:14-15). Later they were famously commissioned to make disciples of all nations (Matthew 28:18-20).

And what about Pentecost? The immediate result of that experience was 3,000 new believers, and the ongoing fruit of that historic encounter is seen in the nations continuing to receive the Gospel to this day. Jesus Himself said that the Holy Spirit would come and we would be His witnesses (Acts 1:8). In Paul's dramatic encounter, he received his commission as apostle to the Gentiles and was given a promise of great suffering (Acts 9:15-16).

I think the pattern is self-evident. Encounter leads to mission. The experience of God's presence thrusts us into the world with His work and His message. It has never been otherwise.

And yet, today we have untold thousands of believers who enjoy the experience of the presence of the Lord every single week, yet who are impotent when it comes to making Him known in a hurting and desperate world. Why? How is this even possible?

I can think of only two possible explanations.

First, perhaps these are not true encounters at all. Maybe we've learned how to manipulate emotions to mimic the feeling of the presence of God, but it's not the real thing. Perhaps the music and the lights and the fog machines and the amazing shows we experience each week provide only faint shadows of what the people of old meant by the presence of God. This would explain why our encounter leads only to a desire for more encounter.

Isaiah did not beg to stay in the heavenly temple. Moses did not build a monastery at the site of the burning bush. Abraham did not return to Ur seeking to hear again the great voice. And yet people leave worship services each week, not longing to take this wondrous power into the darkness around, but only looking forward to the next experience.

But maybe I'm too cynical. I do confess that is my unfortunate tendency. Maybe these are genuine encounters with the Almighty. Maybe what we feel in these gatherings is the God of Pentecost coming again among His people. But if so, we must face the other possibility.

We love the feeling of His presence, but we simply do not love Jesus.

Jesus said that the way we show that we love Him is to obey Him. His purpose in meeting with us is to send us into the world with His message and His power and His love. Perhaps He has other purposes, but it is never less than this, unless He has changed since the days of scripture. So He faithfully meets with us, even allowing us an experience of His touch and His presence, and in that moment we are filled with the power of the Holy Spirit to be His witnesses. But we don't do anything about it. We just live our lives. Our disobedience is brazen. Surrounding ourselves with Christian friends and Christian businesses and Christian coffee shops and Christian music and Christian lives that are insulated from the world He longs to reach.

Of course, there is still hope for us in Jesus. How amazing that He still gifts us with His presence, and still speaks to us, and still invites us and calls us into something more. The hope is that it is the power of the Holy Spirit that makes us witnesses. The hope is that we can still say Yes to Him. We can still encounter Him.

25 BE WEAK

"But he said to me, 'My grace is sufficient for you, for my power is made perfect in weakness.' Therefore I will boast all the more gladly about my weaknesses, so that Christ's power may rest on me. That is why, for Christ's sake, I delight in weaknesses, in insults, in hardships, in persecutions, in difficulties. For when I am weak, then I am strong." -- 2 Corinthians 12:9-10

"And so it was with me, brothers and sisters. When I came to you, I did not come with eloquence or human wisdom as I proclaimed to you the testimony about God. For I resolved to know nothing while I was with you except Jesus Christ and him crucified. I came to you in weakness with great fear and trembling." -- 1 Corinthians 2:1-3

It was a 'typical' summer missions trip, if there is any such thing. We were in Uganda with a team of short-term missionaries from all over the US. We had been in the country long enough for some of the excitement to wear off, and for the work to feel more grueling than inspiring. I was beginning to hear complaints and to see people slack off in their effort. Team members were getting testy with one another. The children's ministry team was feeling dubious of their long-term impact. The construction team was tired and thinking they may not finish their objectives. The evangelism group wasn't sure how they felt about things. I had taken a moment to step away from the team, and found a refreshing patch of shade in which to sit and pray. "*I delight in weakness.*"

Wait a minute! That's us! We are weak. We are feeling like this is hard and that we don't know what we're doing. We are feeling spent -- physically, emotionally, spiritually. *This is wonderful!*

There will be no long-term fruit in your mission or outreach until you become weak. Until it gets too hard for you. Until you cannot figure out how to do it. Until you become convinced that the task is too much for you, that you are too small, too insignificant, too foolish, too frail. Until you can say, and know the truth of it from the depths of your heart, "I can't make it! I can't succeed. I'm too weak." And then look to Jesus. It has to get beyond the place of mere mental assent. You have to know this with all your soul as an agonizing and desperate reality.

As you have prepared for this mission, or engaged in this outreach, I'm guessing you've put some thought into your strengths, your gifts, what you have to offer. Cool. Maybe you've talked about them as a team, or listed them when you applied to be part of this whole deal. But now that's all out the window. Your strengths are not getting it done. You've done some good of course. You've encouraged or helped in some physical way or shared some truth or given a child a happy few hours. But you're wondering what the long-term, even eternal, fruit will be of all this.

For when I am weak, then I am strong.

God made you strong in certain ways, and He has given you gifts and abilities and talents. And He has called you to submit these to Him that He can use them for the glory of Jesus. And you are doing that. You're giving your all. Way to go. Seriously. But it's not enough. He has also made you weak. Dependent. Not sufficient by yourself. He created you to need Him and to need others.

Your weakness opens the door for the power of God to work through you. Your inability makes way for His ability. Your lack is the very door for His provision. Once you experience the reality that apart from Him you can do nothing (John 15:5), you will be able to experience the reality of His power being made perfect in your weakness. You have known this, theoretically. But there is something about experiencing the raw reality of your weakness that is essential to experiencing the reality of His power.

Weakness has another essential power, too. It binds you as a team in a way that your strengths never can. Your weakness carries the potential for vulnerability. And vulnerability carries the potential for true relationship. Focusing on your strengths sets you apart. Focusing on your weaknesses brings you together.

This is such good news, friends! Be weak!

I came to you in weakness with great fear and trembling. It might take a little time, but once you get to that place, you are really in business. Once you become absolutely convinced that your strength won't get it done, and that you are simply not enough, things will begin to happen. When you hit that moment of "Oh-my-goodness-what-have-I-gotten-myself-into-I-can't-do-this," you will find yourself in the same place as the apostle Paul as he entered the great city of Corinth. Fear. Trembling. Weakness. These are the materials Jesus can work with. Not the fear of pain or death, or the fear of failure, or the fear of punishment, but the fear that comes from a thorough understanding of your own insufficiency.

We are obsessed with our gifts. Paul was much more impressed by his weaknesses. A few years ago, I wrote the following reflection after a Thursday Night dinner with the homeless:

I hate conflict. I hate violence. I'm not talking about in the "I think violence is wrong and I hate that it occurs" stream, though that is true, too. But I'm talking much more self-centered here. I hate being around even the hint of violence. It makes me... uncomfortable. Honestly, it makes me scared. And not just violence. Loud arguments. Threats. Tension. Confrontation. Makes my stomach turn.

So, Owen Park this week was... stretching. And beautiful! Oh, so beautiful! When I first became aware of the problem, it seemed to be escalating fast...

A group of people -- mostly regulars -- are sitting at a table eating. There is one newcomer in their midst, a young Native American. Suddenly, in a flurry of profanities and threats, one of the regulars is jumping to his feet and pulling off his jacket, pointing menacingly towards the newbie.

Gulp. I look around. Crud. Where's Jesse when I need him? He always handled this stuff so freaking well. None of the others on the team tonight seem to be aware of this growing conflict. I take a deep breath and utter a desperate prayer. I timidly step up to the man, who is now standing threateningly over the youngster, and still shouting profanities. 'Excuse me, we need to not do this here. Umm.. This is a family event.' Blah blah blah. I feel like a dork. Fortunately, the man's friends are gathering around him now, and leading him away. 'But that one's the problem,' they all assure me. 'He keeps running his mouth, and asking for trouble.'

Our young friend has been sitting quietly through all of this, but now he erupts. More profanities. More threats. 'If I had my knife...' Blah blah blah.

Deep breath. Desperate prayer. I sit down across the table from the enraged youth. 'Hi, my name is Tim.' I offer my hand. I again feel like an idiot. I see him kind of shake his head. Something changes. His eyes focus.

'I'm Freddie.' We shake hands.

Ok. good start.

'I'm kinda buzzed right now.'

I nod. That at least seems clear enough.

'I'm glad you came tonight man,' I boldly lie.

'Are you the church?' he queries.

'Yes, we are.'

'I used to go to church. I used to be a Christian. I loved Jesus. I still love Jesus, but I do bad things...' and Freddie sits there and tells me of his life of pain, rejection, disappointment. He tells me about the drugs and the heart-break of his girl-friend breaking up with him. He tells me about his former life in a youth group, loving Jesus and living for Him. About wanting to be good. About the pain. He keeps coming back to the pain.

I find myself in the familiar situation of not knowing what to say, not knowing how to comfort or speak truth or show love or offer grace. Not knowing how to represent Jesus. So I listen and share a few words, and repeat often that God does care and it's not too late and He still loves you.

After about twenty minutes the conversation winds down, and I offer to pray. Reaching across the table, I touch Freddie, and ask Jesus to comfort him, and to reveal Himself to him. And I tell him, truthfully, that I'm really glad he came tonight, and that I hope he comes back next week.

And this is how it ends tonight. In my greatest weakness, the Lord shows Himself strong again. In the midst of my fear and insecurity, Jesus brings calm and peace. And He really does love Freddie. And there really is hope for Freddie, because there is hope for me. And it's ok to not be full of confidence and ease. It's ok to be afraid sometimes. 'I was with you in weakness, in fear, and in much trembling.'

I have failed in ministry more gloriously than I have succeeded. I am still frustrated by the things I cannot seem to do, no matter how hard I try. Sometimes I decide to grit my teeth and find a way to do it myself. But at other times, I get desperate in prayer, and I look for friends to help me. And I hit the jackpot.

26 PLOD

William Carey is often referred to as 'The Father of Modern Missions.' He left his British home in 1793 to become a missionary in India, where he served until his death 41 years later. The list of accomplishments during his missionary service is remarkable, although he faced extreme trials. He once lost ten years of translation work in a devastating fire, only to start over the following day. In the end, he provided his own analysis regarding the reason for his success:

> "If after my removal any one should think it worth his while to write my Life, I will give you a criterion by which you may judge of its correctness. If he give me credit for being a plodder he will describe me justly. Anything beyond this will be too much. I can plod. I can persevere in any definite pursuit. To this I owe everything."[17]

Centuries earlier, the writer of Hebrews encouraged the scattered tribes of Israel with these words,

> "You need to persevere so that when you have done the will of God, you will receive what he has promised." -- Hebrews 10:36

---

[17] George Smith, *The Life of William Carey, D.D.: Shoemaker and Missionary* (London: John Murray, 1885), vii.

I had been serving in Uganda for two years when I wrote a letter that could have marked the end of my missionary work. I was depressed, frightened, lonely, and just done. For months I had agonized over what to do. I had repeatedly poured out my woes to my wife and felt desperate for something to change. The letter was written to John Taylor, the new director of our missions organization. In it, I expressed my feelings and recounted my failures. I suggested that I was not fit for missionary life and concluded by requesting to be released from my commitment. I wanted to go home. I longed to just quit. To never again attempt something so lofty and so beyond my abilities. I sent the letter, eagerly awaiting the reply that would set off a welcomed flurry of activity -- packing, purchasing plane tickets, making new plans.

Instead, the reply was a thoughtful but impassioned call to persevere. "Give it one more year." John understood that the Christian life -- let alone missionary service -- could simply be hard. Character is built through sticking with the tough stuff.

"Not only so, but we also glory in our sufferings, because we know that suffering produces perseverance; perseverance, character; and character, hope." Romans 5:3-4

By the grace of God, I recognized the spark of wisdom in John's letter. I began to see my situation through new eyes, and everything changed. I am so thankful that he did not simply agree with me, coddle me, give in to me. He challenged me to face reality. Reality is that life includes struggle. If we desire to bear fruit for the Kingdom, we must face the facts of suffering and hardship. We must be determined to stick to it when we do not want to. We have to be willing to stubbornly stay. Sometimes we are simply required to stand. Do not give up.

> "Endure suffering along with me, as a good soldier of Christ Jesus." -- 2 Timothy 2:3 (NLT)

At some point, your weekly outreach or your missions trip or your church ministry will get hard. It may get really, really hard. Further along, you will want to stop. The motivation that once came so easily will vanish, and every movement will require a supreme effort. You may think things like, "I no longer have the grace for this" (whatever that means) or "I think God is calling me to move on." And maybe He is. But not because it's hard.

> "They [Paul and Barnabas] encouraged them to continue in the faith, reminding them that we must suffer many hardships to enter the Kingdom of God." -- Acts 14:22 (NLT)

I have often become discouraged in the ministry of Thursday Night Light. I cannot tell you the number of times I have dreaded the trek over to 3rd and Detroit on a Thursday evening. In such times, the thought that I don't have to do this anymore makes my heart leap. Nobody is forcing me to do this. I can just stop. Seriously. Freedom! But, by the grace of God, something has always checked this downward spiral before it gets too far. The truth is, I must continue, regardless of my feelings -- even if those feelings persist over a long period of time. This is not about my fulfillment or my value or even my gifts. It is a matter of calling and a matter of obedience and a matter of living for the glory of God above all else.

The level of hardship is not a valid consideration in determining your involvement in any Kingdom pursuit. It is simply and fully irrelevant. That can be a hard pill to swallow for American believers like us. But we must. This includes reaching out on mission and it includes serving in your local church and it includes personal disciplines in spiritual growth.

"If I wonder why something trying is allowed, and press for prayer that it may be removed; if I cannot be trusted with any disappointment, and cannot go on in peace under any mystery, then I know nothing of Calvary love." — Amy Carmichael[18]

If you will take hold of this conviction -- that hardship is simply a part of the game -- it will help you to persevere. It will defend you from the mind games that lead to quitting and giving up. It will enable you to plod.

Plod. Such an unimpressive, uninspiring word. Boring. Even depressing. Who wants to be known as a plodder? But there is a great secret here, and I urge you to not miss it. Carey was onto something big. If we will just put ourselves in the position for God to do something, believe in His power and His purpose, and hold on until we see it happen, I believe we will see wonderful things. Too often we quit before He is ready to advance. Too often we decide the whole thing was a mistake, robbing Him of the opportunity to use us.

Quitting can happen on more than one level. You may be on an overseas mission trip, and quitting in the sense of just going home isn't really a valid option. But you can check out. You can stop giving it your all. You can decide to not be fully invested. Or you can simply allow yourself to slide into apathy and laziness. *Persevere!* Your team may not be as awesome as

---

[18] Amy Carmichael, *If* (Christian Literature Crusade, 1938), p 16.

you once thought. *Persevere!* Your leader may have turned into a controlling, insensitive jerk. *Persevere!* The service activities may not be what you had in mind, and the ministry may seem useless or just too hard. Stick with it. Give it your all. You may be exhausted or bored or frustrated or frightened. You may be sick. God is working in ways of which you are completely unaware. Don't give up. William Carey plodded for 41 years. You can, by the grace of God, plod for a few months or a few years.

Maybe you are trying to be part of a weekly outreach, but you find yourself getting busier and busier, and it's just so much easier to not show up. You can convince yourself that you are really not needed, or that you are not appreciated. You can just believe that you are not making a difference. Please, persevere.

Perhaps your engagement in spiritual family (your local church) is waning. You are not satisfied there. You're not being fed. The gathering times are inconvenient. The programs are not what you need. You are busy. You are tired. You're not sure that they still need you or appreciate you or have anything to offer you. I urge you to get back in the game.

We are becoming a society where faithfulness over the long haul is a declining virtue. If we are not careful, it will lose its value altogether and we will cease to recognize it as an essential and godly trait. We're becoming flaky. The best way to overcome this is for us to be faithful in all the little things to which we commit. Be faithful to be all there for the two week or two month mission trip. Be faithful to that weekly outreach. Stick with your community. Pete Greig puts it like this:

> We are strengthened and matured by seasons of boredom and even pain that demands perseverance. In fact, it is

often during these unglamorous, in-between times that we mature; our faith fills up into faithfulness, we learn to push into community and into God's presence, which is, after all, the greatest miracle of all.[19]

I have found that good things tend to happen if we weather the storms and hang in there. God is doing something in us that He will eventually do through us for the sake of others. The doing "in" us can be really hard. And it can take a long time. But hang in there. Be steady. I never know which Thursday night might prove to be one of those times when God breaks through in an obvious and powerful way. Most weeks, it's just plain ole Thursday dinner. We arrive and mill around for a few minutes. We gather a scattering of people to discuss the Bible, and it's generally... ok. Sometimes it's terrible. We circle up, pray, and begin serving food. We sit and have a conversation or two that don't seem to go anywhere significant. We clean up. We say good night. Mundane. Ho hum. But sometimes... Oh man, sometimes something happens. The Father makes Himself known. In the midst of a conversation, you realize God is penetrating a heart. You get to pray for someone, and God touches them. A person comes to repentance, weeping and confessing sin. And you know that all the dozens of normal, nothing special evenings have led to this moment. And you would have missed it if you'd not shown up, because you really didn't want to show up this time. You didn't think this would be one of those nights, and you were convinced it wouldn't really matter if you were there or not.

Persevere.

---

[19] Pete Greig, *Dirty Glory* (Colorado Springs: Navpress, 2016), p 87.

27 GOD'S FAMILY

The family of God is a real and beautiful thing. Many of us tend to think of it in very abstract terms. It is the worldwide people of God. Yep, it is. It consists of all believers of all times and all places. True enough. It is eternal and universal. Absolutely. It is organic.

But we must wrestle with this: The Church is expressed through the local and concrete. It is specific people in a particular place. It has organization and structure. It gathers together for distinct purposes and it has a discernible mission. It has leadership. It has definable boundaries -- you can be inside of it or or outside of it, and you can know which you are.

We talk a lot today about being relational and about having community. We have mentors and coaches, and we have friends.

We have prayer movements and we have mission movements. We have Bible studies and worship sets.

But do we have church? Do we have what the first believers modeled for us? We have many of the activities of church: evangelism and prayer and worship and teaching. We try to fulfill the functions of church -- discipleship and extending the Kingdom. But we do so in a way that does not resemble the first churches. And we are missing out.

Community. Friends. Prayer movements. Worship sets. Bible studies. They are all good, and I don't want to take them away. But there is more! You need more, and you can have more. In fact, if you are going to change the world, you must have more.

Not more as in, *one more thing I should be doing*. But more as in *different*. *Enhanced*. In fact, being part of an actual church family will help to reduce some of that scattered busyness that we confuse for spirituality and mission. It provides focus. It's an all-in-one.

You can have -- you *must* have -- more than a community of friends. You need a family of brothers and sisters. You can have more than teachers and mentors. You require fathers and mothers. You need more than segregated movements and activities. You are offered an integrated life that includes it all.

"Even if you had ten thousand guardians in Christ, you do not have many fathers, for in Christ Jesus I became your father through the gospel." -- 1 Corinthians 4:15

Many of you are living scattered lives. You are consumers of spiritual experience. You do prayer with this set of folks, mission with another, teaching via podcasts from your favorite guru, and maybe hang out socially with another group. Or, if it is all combined in one, full-package group of wonderful people, you insist that it must be only organic, not organizational. It must be free-flowing, not structured. Come and go (of course, as led by the Spirit), but no commitment. Do what you think best, but no submission. No expectations. You "welcome" all, but in reality only accept those like you to be part of the inner circle.

If this is your life, *you are not being discipled*. Jesus did not inaugurate a prayer movement and a missions movement and a discipleship movement. He launched a Kingdom that encompasses them all, and is expressed through local churches. Paul's method of discipleship was simple. Local churches. Churches that were families of believers, filled with the Holy Spirit, entrusted with the Word of God, and mandated to proclaim the Gospel and make disciples.

I have a radical proposal for you. Why can't your real, distinct, local spiritual family be your house of prayer and your mission organization and your community?

You have chosen Kingdom passions and God has given you world-changing dreams. You are ready to sacrifice all and to spend yourself for the mission of Jesus. I sincerely honor you for this. Your vision inspires me. But I have to plead with you: *Don't try this alone.* Don't think your loose and unstructured group of friends will get you there. You have to have the church. The real, visible, local, church. Not a building and not a corporation, but a spiritual family.

I need to add a disclaimer here. When I say church, I am not referring to a place you go on Sunday mornings to sing a few songs, watch the gifted ones minister, write a check, hug a couple of people, and then go out to lunch. Maybe you do gather on Sunday mornings, worship, receive teaching, give, and have some fellowship. But that is only a couple of hours in a full week of life and ministry together.

Part of the issue, of course, is that we have allowed church to become something it was never meant to be. An organization that is there to take care of me and meet my spiritual needs. Floyd McClung makes this claim:

"Millions of Christians have given up on traditional church, not because the church demands too much of them, but because it demands too little. The church in the

West is stuck in a rut of building-based, Sunday-centric, pastor-oriented Christianity."[20]

But the church is so much more! You know these people and are known by them. You serve together, and the unique part you bring is needed. You are loved. You belong. You hang out together and dream together and pray together and serve together and proclaim the Gospel together. You encourage one another and correct one another and support one another and take care of one another.

Of course -- and here's where it gets tough -- the church is also other things. It is a family that fully includes every ridiculously awkward and embarrassing schmuck that shows up. It welcomes that annoying and full-of-herself mom with her bratty kids. The argumentative theology student, the lazy millennial, the over-enthusiastic vegan evangelist, and the pyramid scheme schemer. It's made up of the carnal hipster clique who spend their time discussing music and movies and drinking beer. The social justice zealot who just wants to stick it to the man. The sickeningly happy dating couple who rarely seem to come up for a breath. It includes the social media whiner and the enraged political activist. The depressed and the anxious. The guy who is negative about everything, and the one who cannot admit to anything but happiness and positivity. People who know nothing about the Bible and scoff at your 'quiet time.' People who know everything about the Bible and love to stuff it down your throat. And it includes you. So deal with it. Seriously. This is family.

When David was on the run from King Saul, the Bible says that "all those who were in distress or in debt or

---

[20] Floyd McClung, *You See Bones, I See an Army* (Seattle: YWAM Publishing, 2007), pg 188.

discontented gathered around him, and he became their commander. About four hundred men were with him." (1 Samuel 22:2). These are the ones God gave David to help him turn the kingdom around. These were his people. Eugene Peterson describes it like this:

> "When we get serious about the Christian life, we eventually end up in a place and among people decidedly uncongenial to what we expected. At least uncongenial to what *I* expected. That place and people is often called a church. It is hard to get over the disappointment that God, having made an exception in my case, didn't seem to call nice, accomplished, courteous, alert people to worship."[21]

We need the local church, if for no other reason, to force us into the messy reality of... reality. You can't just live your life with the awesome people, the people who agree with you, the theologically correct, the fully compatible, the spiritually mature, the *this-is-the-best-family-ever-s*. You need the ordinary run-of-the-mill rascals like us. Because these are the ones Jesus uses to change the freaking world.

Think about the following questions:
* With whom did you take your last missions trip?
* With whom did you participate in your last local outreach?
* Who do you hang out with when you have leisure time?
* Who do you turn to when you need something?
* What biblical teacher has the most influence on you?
* Who counsels you when you are hurting / confused / in need of direction?

---

[21] Eugene Peterson, *The Pastor* (Harper Collins ebooks, 2011), p 106.

* With whom do you mostly pray?

If the answer to most of these questions has nothing to do with your local church, let me suggest some re-alignment work. Your foundation may be off. You are surrounded by people, but you are in fact a loner. You decide which ministries you participate in. You decide what teachings you want to hear. You decide who to hang out with and where to get help. You are in control. You're living like you have no family. Like an orphan.

Now, maybe you are in college or a discipleship program, and you have been engaging in the above activities through various campus ministries and outreaches. That is really good, and it is what God is using for you in this season. But it is temporary. One day you are going to move out of the dorms and the training wheels will come off. And you will need the church. Because of the powerful experiences you have now, be determined not to settle for something inferior in your next season. Understand that the church is the long-term solution. You need it!

"But I'm doing great!" My life is fruitful! I'm loving Jesus and making Him known!" I know! Way to go! But what if I told you that you could bring even more glory to the Father? And that what you're doing apart from the local church is unsustainable? There will be cracks. Your work will be unstable. I am talking about so much more than a "spiritual covering." More than finding a church to attend regularly because you have to. More than getting a local church pastor to say that they like what you're doing, and will try and support and help you. I am talking about an all-of-life walk with the same people for a long time.

In order for this family to truly be what you need to change the world, consider the following four characteristics. These are not meant to be the definition of a church, but these must be included if this is going to work in the long term.

First, there must be **commitment**. This is not a situation where you can just show up when you want, give according to your mood, and serve however you feel led. There are *expectations* that become priorities in your life. You are counted on. Your engagement is required. You are needed at specific times and for specific events. You will re-orient your life around this family and its God-given mission. You are committed to this group of people, and you will not abandon them when relationships become difficult, when you don't get to use your gifts as you desire, or when you've found a better group. This ceases to be about you and your needs, and you realize you are in something for the long haul that is bigger than you. Of course, you may eventually leave -- but you will be sent out intentionally for the sake of the Kingdom, not simply wander off to a new thing. Church is not meant to be easy.

> "The modern church has made the Christian life way too easy for its members. This has marginally increased the numbers attending our churches, but we're fairly certain it has caused many more problems than it solved."[22]

Secondly, there must be **leadership**. The New Testament church is led by elders. This is family language. It speaks to the maturity and experience of those who lead. This is no random, unstructured group of friends. Families have moms and dads. There is order. There are different roles that must

---

[22] David Watson and Paul Watson, *Contagious Disciple Making* (Nashville: Thomas Nelson, 2014), p 40.

be filled. There are those who have been given responsibility for the family -- though in another sense all are responsible together. Yes, there is equality of value and equality of belonging. Absolutely. This is essential! But not everyone has the same role or exercises the same authority. This is also key. Study the New Testament, and you can't miss this.

Many of you have mentors and teachers that are wonderful and whom you greatly respect. They care for you and support you and encourage you. But they only know, for the most part, what you tell them. I'm sure you're honest and open, but it's still just your perspective. They do have the insight of the Holy Spirit, which is truly powerful. But the Father has made you for family. Fathers and mothers are those who see your messy bedroom and know what time you got home last night. They know if you are lazy or diligent, reliable or flaky. And they still love you and believe in you.

Thirdly, there must be **submission**. You are called to entrust yourself to this family. They must be able to hold you accountable, and even to discipline you when needed. They can correct and rebuke, and you are committed to humbly submitting. Of course, this is a *mutual* submission. You are part of the group that the others are submitting to as well. Even leaders -- *especially leaders* -- submit to the group as a whole, and can be called to account.

I serve in leadership with a group of elders in a local church. Although I am the senior leader in the group, I am submitted to the others. I promise them, for example, that I will not leave the church to pursue a different ministry or vocation or location, unless the elders agree with me that this is what God is calling me to do. Does that feel risky? Absolutely. I'm trusting my life to them! But in reality they are my safety net. They will not allow me to jump ship based on anything less than God's call. I need that.

Finally, I urge you to ensure there is a common *purpose*. You are committed, there is leadership, and you are submitted because there is something bigger than you at stake. All of you are unified in the conviction that this family exists, not to just care for and love one another, but to make the Gospel known and to invite in and welcome the Father's lost ones. You are determined to find your mission together, and to pursue it with all your heart. You submit individual dreams and aspirations, only to see them enlarged as you throw them in the mix with everyone else's. You are "striving together as one for the faith of the gospel." (Philippians 1:27).

So, attach yourself to a local church. Remember that your church is more a matter of a calling than a choice. It is more about service than preference. Let your roots go down deep in the good soil of spiritual family. Don't settle for a church to attend. Find a family to join. Take the risk. Please.

28 FAMILY OR MISSION?

Spiritual family is truly powerful. But you also have another family. You've got a 'physical family' -- a dad and mom, brothers and sisters. Maybe a husband or wife and a few kids. Or maybe you will one day. And when that day comes, you will be confronted with some pretty serious priority issues. How does your radical life of discipleship and mission fit in with your responsibilities of leading a family?   Or are they even compatible? Maybe the radical stuff was for your youth, and now it's time to get on with the serious business of responsible living. A lot of people take that route. Or maybe you can simply keep doing what you've always done, and hope that your family can keep up, reminding them to make sacrifices for the Kingdom. Others have done this as well.

"My family is my biggest priority."   That's responsible. Wisdom.

> "If anyone comes to me and does not hate father and mother, wife and children, brothers and sisters—yes, even their own life—such a person cannot be my disciple." Heretic! Oh wait, that was Jesus (Luke 14:26). Awkward.

So... Abandon our families and give all our available time instead to outward ministry?

157

"If anyone does not know how to manage his own family, how can he take care of God's church?" -- 1 Timothy 3:5

I'm guessing that managing involves time.

So what are we to do? If you are young and do not yet have a family, I have to tell you this: If you fail to get this issue of family and ministry right, it will very likely derail the very kingdom ambitions God has put in your heart. By 'getting it right,' I do not mean perfection in all the details. Trust me, it will be messy, and you will learn some tough lessons the hard way. But I do mean developing a biblical understanding and endeavoring to live that out in all facets of life, though you will often blow it. If you do have a family, and have felt this tension already, I'd like to offer some encouragement, and perhaps exhortation.

Francis Chan gives us something to think about:

"Can you really call your marriage 'good' if your focus on your family keeps you from making disciples, caring for the poor, reaching out to the lost, and using your talents and resources for others?"[23]

So, let's consider this question: How do you live up to biblical standards of family and mission without compromising either? Is that even possible? Mike and Sally Breen argue that we do this by integrating the two in what can be a beautifully seamless way of life:

If we're going to make disciples and move out in mission, we need to go from managing boundaries between the compartments of our lives to integrating family and

---

[23] Francis and Lisa Chan, *You and Me Forever* (San Francisco: Claire Love Publishing, 2014), Kindle Location 1272.

mission into one life, a cohesive framework and fabric that empowers a culture of discipleship and mission, not just occasional events and periodic programs.[24]

Our western Christian culture has convinced us that family is the ultimate; the highest priority of life. To many, even our Master and His mission must bow to this supreme responsibility. We believe this, even though Jesus Himself challenges us to put Him above all earthly ties, including family.

My answer to the "how" question is two-fold, and quite simple. It is not meant to be thorough, and may well cause more questions. That's great. My admonition to you is to not just let it happen thoughtlessly. Pursue God's heart in this, begging Him for wisdom and courage.

First, include your family in your mission. Of course, you most likely cannot do this always, or even most of the time. But you can make a habit of it whenever possible, even if it does seem to limit you in some ways, or cause inconvenience. There are so many ways you can do this. Be creative!

I have a friend who took each of his children on a mission trip with him (or his wife) when they turned 13. The child chose the destination, and was involved in the ministry. One of his daughters chose Sudan, and they worked it out so they could spend a couple of days with my family and me in Uganda on the way. The daughter actively served with her dad during their short stay with us, and I was deeply impacted.

When we lived in Uganda, I took each of our kids on ministry trips within the country, and on occasion we went as a whole family. They were able to experience what was a big part of my life -- traveling in the bush, staying with hospitable

---

[24] Mike and Sally Breen, *Family on Mission* (2014), p 47.

local pastors, and ministering to people. I remember taking my son Nathan with me for a few days to a remote village in the mountains when he was six years old. I had been to this particular place a number of times over the years, but it was the first time I had brought any of my children. The sight of a white child was such a novelty that a small crowd of people instantly gathered anytime we stepped outside. Even our trips to the latrine became a not-to-be-missed spectacle. Nathan took it all surprisingly well and it created a fantastic bonding experience for us, the memories of which I treasure to this day.

These days, living in Tulsa, involving our kids is still a priority. I've been able to travel internationally with three of them on mission trips. More than that, they have all been frequent participants in our Thursday night dinner for the homeless during different seasons. I remember an occasion looking across the crowded parking lot, trying to locate my teenage son. I eventually discovered him, seated on the short wall that borders the lot, in earnest conversation with an older homeless man -- dirty and rough looking. Joy flooded my heart in that moment. Yes, I am sure that their discussion was often awkward, and sprinkled with profanities and vulgarity. But my son was, out of love for Jesus, engaging with the lost and broken. Since then, it's become a familiar sight. My boys can often be found on a Thursday evening, sitting and sharing a meal and conversation with the poor. My little ones like to come as well, and my friends from the street often express disappointment when I'm alone. "Where are the kids tonight?" they ask with a note of disapproving rebuke.

I also share with my family my ups and downs and struggles in the ministry, as appropriate. They pray for me and encourage me. The older ones will text to ask me how a certain appointment went, or check in on me after an important event.

Of course, I can make this all appear very straightforward and rosy. And obviously it's just not. Sometimes I get more and more caught up in stuff, and I neglect giving my wife and kids the time and attention they need and deserve. Sometimes I miss it by neglecting an important ministry opportunity because I just want to be with my family, and I don't make the sacrifice. Other times, my kids get angry when I go out in an evening. "You're *never* home." They have no idea how such indictments sting. Too often I return to the family at the end of the day, exhausted, and don't give them my energy or attention, because I am consumed with myself and my desire to do nothing. But even so, involving my family in mission is important, and is bearing good fruit.

Secondly, in addition to involving my family in ministry, it is crucial to invite ministry into my family. It's a two-way street. My family goes with me in outreach. And I invite the people that I pastor and the ones I am trying to reach into my family. I do not do this near as well as I want, and we are working on it, but it is powerful.

I've listened to many preachers over the years, and been impressed by their messages and their stories. But I have no way of knowing how they actually live it all out. Are they genuine? I believe so. I hope so. Does it really work the way they suggest it might? I am intrigued by the scripture I quoted earlier:

"If anyone does not know how to manage his own family, how can he take care of God's church?" -- 1 Timothy 3:5

How would anyone know if these potential elders were managing their own families well? They must have had access on a pretty intimate level. My sermons are not particularly powerful, and my writing does not inspire great movements of transformation. But, if Christ is real in me, my life, weighty with the fruit of the Spirit, must make a difference. "Be an example!" Paul exhorts Timothy (1 Tim 4:12). How can he be an example unless people see -- really see -- his life?

My home must be a place of significant ministry. It may in fact be the most significant place of ministry I ever have. My living room carries more potential for impact than a stage in an auditorium ever could. But there is a problem here.

We Americans value privacy. My space. The place where I can control what goes on. A place where I can let my hair down and stop having to perform and be something special. A sanctuary where I can be refreshed after my day-long battles in the world. Me-time. We all need it, right? We value these ideals so highly, in fact, that they have become sacred. Many of us are convinced that they originate in the Bible. But, to be honest, they stem from our culture. The wisdom of the world. As followers of Jesus who long to see His Kingdom in our communities and in the nations, we need to shift our thinking. Our exalting of the idea of privacy and personal space has robbed the church of one of its greatest assets: your home and your family.

I grew up in what I have since discovered was a highly unusual setting. Years before I was born, my dad started the "Trosdale Home for Boys." A few years later, he married my mom, and together they sought to provide a home for boys who were lost in the foster care system. They typically had around a dozen boys (sometimes more), ages 8-18, living with them. I was born into this large and diverse family, and lived there until I was almost eight years old. After an interim period when another couple ran the home, my oldest brother took over. My parents offered the most powerful thing they had to give to the boys who came under their care -- family. We took vacations together, celebrated holidays together, ate meals together, went to school together, and played together. We fought and struggled and learned together. Even after we moved out, our home -- just a few miles away -- was an important part in the lives of many of these "Trosdale brothers." It often happened that one or two of them were around. Sometimes for a day or a few days. Some for weeks or months or years. My parents traded in their "right" to privacy and control for an opportunity to change lives and offer the gift of family. I experienced the difficulties of this first-hand -- and believe me, they were profound. But I also see the fruit of it to this day.

When we lived in Uganda, we quickly learned that our friends who were pastors considered their homes a central place of ministry. It seemed more common for people in need of counsel or prayer or financial help to look for their pastor at his residence than at the church building where they worshiped. If we were to be effective there, we learned that our home would have to be a similar place of hospitality and ministry. Upon leaving Uganda, many friends gave speeches to appreciate and bless us as we went. I often listened in vain to hear how my teaching or my "official" ministry brought transformation or blessing to people. However, I did often hear about how our home had made a difference.

In the States, it sometimes feels less natural. We are living in the midst of people who love privacy to the point of idolatry. And yet, what a powerful opportunity we have! As I mentioned, we are still learning how to do this better and recognize that we have a long way to go. Still, we have seen the power in sharing holiday meals with many different people

-- from neighbors who are good friends to college students from out of town to a homeless family with nowhere to go. Our church family spends a lot of time in our home (and we in theirs). Our kids cannot escape our ministry even when they are not going "out" with us. Most of the time, they like it. It causes inconveniences for sure. They have to share their space. And their toys. But they know they are involved in the work of the Kingdom. And that is priceless.

Take your family with you as you minister, creating special family times together. Welcome people into your home, and allow them to see how you relate to your spouse and your kids. Your outreach and your living room are probably the two most powerful contexts you have for discipleship -- both of your own family, and of others the Lord gives you to serve.

Let's leave behind the "family vs ministry" fallacy. I hope we can blur our boundary lines to the extent that we don't know where one begins and the other ends. God has given you family. God has given you a mission. Not only are these compatible, but they are integral parts of one another.

29 TO NARNIA AND BACK

"Dearest," said Aslan very gently, "you and your brother will never come back to Narnia"

"Oh, *Aslan*!!" said Edmond and Lucy together in despairing voices.

"You are too old, children," said Aslan, "and you must begin to come close to your own world now."

"It isn't Narnia, you know," sobbed Lucy. It's *you*. We shan't meet *you* there. And how can we live, never meeting you?"

"But you shall meet me, dear one." said Aslan.

"Are – are you there, too, Sir?" said Edmond.

"I am," said Aslan. "But there I have another name. You must learn to know me by that name. This was the very reason why you were brought to Narnia, that by knowing me here for a little, you may know me better there."[25]

Short-term mission trips can sometimes seem like an adventure in Narnia, C.S. Lewis' magical land where ordinary children become heroes and great kings and queens. For a couple of weeks you not only step into another world altogether, in some ways it seems you become a different

---

[25] C.S. Lewis, *The Voyage of the Dawn Treader* (New York: HarperTrophy Publishers, 1952), p 247.

person. Bolder. More compassionate. More zealous. More alive. More spiritual. Better. And it just seems like Jesus is right there. You feel His presence. You hear Him talking to you. Worship is amazing. Prayer actually seems to get through. That guy with the migraine even got healed when you prayed for him – right on the spot. And those two high school girls who gave their hearts to Jesus when you shared with them! You'll never forget that. Or maybe you simply had amazing conversations about Jesus with complete strangers – and you hardly ever even do that with your own husband. But, that was all in "Narnia," and now you're headed back to your cubicle or your classroom or your dad's house or the job or wherever, and it's just a tad bit different. But there is great news. Having experienced more of Jesus *here*, you can live more fully in Him *there*. That's one of the reasons He sent you. Not the only reason for sure – but definitely one reason.

If I were to ask you today if you have experienced a transformation through your mission or local outreach that would continue in your life *there*, most likely you'd say, "definitely!." But what if I ask the same question in just a few days from now? What about three months from now? Or better yet – what if I asked your spouse? Your parents? Your friends? Would they confirm that something is different in you? It's not automatic. It *is* very possible. The *potential* for lasting change is there. The seeds have been sown deep in your heart -- but will they grow? You want them to – but honestly it can seem a little hopeless. Life back home is just so... *normal*. But take heart in this – God sent you to Narnia, and you can be pretty sure that one of the reasons He sent you was to bring about some change in you. God's on your side in this: *"being confident of this, that he who began a good work in you will carry it on to completion until the day of Christ Jesus."* (Philippians

1:6). Yes! Those seeds of change in your life can grow into an abundant harvest for the glory of Jesus. Here are a few thoughts as to how you can help that to happen:

First, *reflect* on the experience. Talk to the Lord about all that happened. Write out your thoughts and prayers in a journal. Write about what God did through you and in you over the past weeks. Do this soon. Take a few quiet evenings, or get away for an entire weekend if you can. Consider some of the following:

- When and how did you see God's hand on this trip or outreach? What did He show you through those times? What does He want you to take from these experiences?

- What were some challenges for you? Why were these things hard? How did you handle them? What is the Lord teaching you through them? What growth would you like to see as a result of passing through these difficulties?

- How does God want you to be different as a result of your journey? Be as specific as you can. Be realistic. Don't expect dramatic changes in every area overnight. Also, don't make too long of a list. Focus on a few significant things.

As part of your reflection time, set some specific goals. Move beyond, "I'm going to pray more," or "I'm going to view material things differently" or "I'm going to be more bold in my witness for Jesus." Try something like, "By God's grace I'm going to get up a half hour earlier every morning for the sake of prayer, and I'm going to begin a prayer journal,..." and "With God's help I'm going to make a budget, and force myself into a simpler lifestyle. I'm going to allot myself no more than $___ per month for entertainment, eating out, etc. And I'm going to give $___ to _____ ministry every month, and I'm going to..." and "I'm going to ask for God's anointing to be a true witness to ___ and ___. I'm going to pray for them every day, and ask for open doors to share God's love with them. I'm going to begin reading my Bible during lunch break at work, and being open to talking to co-workers about what I'm reading. And I will..." Write out these goals, and put them somewhere where you will read them often. Keep them before your eyes.

Secondly, *don't do this alone.* Share with a trusted friend. It would be great if you can do so with someone who was on the trip with you, or is part of your regular outreach. Even before leaving the field, find someone to be an accountability and encouragement partner. Or gather a group of three or four. Many of your teammates will be having the same longing for real transformation as you. Take advantage of the moment. It'll be harder to take this step once you're home. Make an appointment now to get together soon. Soon. Do it soon. Even if you live far away, you can make it work. Be determined. Share the results of your reflection times, and check up on each other. Pray together. Ask how things are going in specific areas. Talk things through. Talk about what God did in you, and some of the challenges you face in living this out back home. Accountability and friendship are terrific things to help keep you going.

Thirdly, *keep ministering.* Make a lifestyle out of putting yourself in stretching situations. Don't sit back on the plane with a big "*Whew!* I did it! Now I can relax a little." What ministry in your local church can you join that will continue to build on your experiences "on missions?" Can you find a

SENT: Reflections for Christians on Mission

ministry that will help you to interact with the poor and the lost and the hurting? Go for it. Maybe you began to experience some of God's burden for children on the trip. Get involved in children's ministry. Sign up and jump in, and trust God to equip you. If He did it in your Narnia, he can do it in Detroit. It may look a little different, but it's *Him* all the same.

And fourthly, *keep the fire burning*. Do all you can do to maintain the new passion that is burning in your heart. Pray. Seek God. Remember this is His work. He's the one giving you the desire to change and to grow.

> For God is working in you, giving you the desire to obey him and the power to do what pleases him. — Philippians 2:13

It's for Him and His glory. Get closer to Jesus. Continually ask Him to share His heart with you; to share His burdens and His joys. Long for His glory. Read your Bible like never before. Try reading Acts and the Gospels over a few times. Get yourself around people who love Jesus and who are living for His glory. Worship Him. Pray. Fast. Be desperate to keep the passion. That's what everything hinges on. I'm not speaking of the emotion – but something deeper than that. The determination. The hunger. The I'm-going-to-hang-onto-this-no-matter-what-it-costs-me.

> Never be lacking in zeal, but keep your spiritual fervor, serving the Lord. Be joyful in hope, patient in affliction, faithful in prayer.
>
> Romans 12:11-12

Therefore, my dear brothers, stand firm. Let nothing move you. Always give yourselves fully to the work of the

Lord, because you know that your labor in the Lord is not in vain.

1 Corinthians 15:58

May God bless you abundantly!

30 YOUR CALL

You've done your outreach for the week, but the next six days count, too. The missions trip is over, but the mission is still on. Love God. Love people. Communicate the Gospel. Be a witness. Touch the poor. Heal the sick. Reach the lost. Be His hands and His feet. Pray. Believe. Your life mission is not fulfilled in a two week stretch one summer – or even a two week stretch *every* summer. It is not fulfilled in a two hour commitment every week. Your mission trips and your outreaches need to become seamless parts of living out your life mission. Too easily in reality they can be just an aberration. A weird aside. A deviation from the normal flow of life. Obviously, in some ways they are that. It's not every day that you're going to share the Gospel with a witchdoctor or get schooled in soccer by twenty bare-foot kids half your size or eat grasshoppers or fix a prostitute's hair or pray for a victim of AIDS. But you are called by God to be on mission everywhere you are, no matter where that is. You're still called to share the Gospel and to reach out to children and to relate to people who are different and to serve the "least of these" and to heal the sick. Pete Greig put it like this:

> "Your call is to feed the hungry and to spend yourself on behalf of the poor... and to offer hospitality to strangers who just turn up in town needing a place to crash. And it's

to fast. And it's to pray so long and hard that you run out of words and tears. Your call is to preach the good news of Jesus to every person who will listen and a few who won't. Your call is to go somewhere, anywhere, wherever, whenever, for Jesus, and never stop. Your call is to love people no one else loves and to forgive them when they treat you like dirt – or worse. Your call is to do your job to the very best of your ability without grumbling about your boss or whining about your colleagues. Your call is to pray for the sick, and when they are healed, to dance all night. And when they are not, to weep with them and love them even more."[26]

A few years ago, I was part of a Bible Study geared towards the lost. After one difficult evening, I wrote this:

Last night I talked to Joe for the first time. Joe is a tough case. I'd seen him around town now and then, and my reaction has been to steer clear of him. Kind of whacked out in the head. Probably on drugs. Abrasive. Hard. That's what I thought of him. So when Tony asked him over to join our Bible Study, I was... well, I was bummed. Tony's been coming to our "journey" Bible Study at a local coffee shop for months now. I love him. He's a good thinker and compassionate and hard-working and a natural leader and just fun to be with. He's still resisting giving his life to Jesus, but I believe he will. He's already challenging us and speaking truth to us on a weekly basis at the Bible Study. I like Tony. It's easy to like Tony. I like talking about Jesus with Tony. This is my kind of evangelism.

[26] Pete Greig, *The Vision and the Vow* (Lake Mary, FL: Relevant Books, 2004), pg 74-75.

But I didn't like Joe. I doubt many people do, to be honest. Except, as my luck would have it, Tony.

So Joe swaggered over and pulled up a chair, and started ranting (that's what I called it to myself) about how the church didn't help him when he needed it, and this and that. We listened. And we listened. And by the end of the night, I was thinking, "What a wasted Bible Study!" AnneMarie invited him back next week. She would. This morning I was praying for the people who come to the Bible Study, and I naturally had to include Joe too. And as I prayed, it hit me that this guy is hurting. He is so bound by the enemy that he can't see reality. He acts tough and like he's something big, but it's all a defense. Inside he's in pain. Oh Jesus! The pain that is in this world!

I believe this morning Jesus let me know that He feels Joe's pain. Every bit of it. And, if I'm willing, He wants to share it with me so that I can feel it too. What a privilege! For Jesus to share with me His pain over one of the lost precious ones that He is seeking. Jesus can yet be glorified in Joe's life.

How do we live missional lives in our normal, everyday world? There are no easy answers to this, but it's worth pursuing. Well worth it, in fact. I'm going to be honest with you. I'm not great at this. I have some friends who are, and they are a constant challenge to me. I miss opportunities all the time. I tend to pray for God to bring me divine appointments, but inwardly hope He won't take me too seriously. But, by the grace of God, I am getting better.

For me, the number one key in living a missional lifestyle is *the grace of God*. It's all Him! It so is. I'm finding that I need to really pray it up if I'm going to be a witness for Jesus. I need to ask Him. I need to go way beyond asking for those divine appointments and open doors. I need to ask Him for the grace to walk through them. I'm a total beggar in this. I have to rely on Him completely, because one thing I know is that I *will* fail on my own. No doubt at all. But I'm becoming desperate for Him to work this in me. Why? What is getting me to this point of desperation? It's love for Him. I want to see His glory. I want Him to get glory through my life and the lives of others. It's what I live for. I am seeking Him and praying and worshiping and loving Him with all that I am. I don't want my life to be wasted one little bit. I want Him to get every drop of glory out of my days that He possibly can. I want to have something to offer Him when I stand before Him in Heaven – as a gift of gratitude and love. The more my eyes are on Jesus, the more I seem to see people. And I see them differently. Like with Joe.

> Such confidence as this is ours through Christ before God. Not that we are competent in ourselves to claim anything for ourselves, but our competence comes from God. He has made us competent as ministers of a new covenant— not of the letter but of the Spirit; for the letter kills, but the Spirit gives life.   1 Corinthians 3:4-6

Again, listen to how Pete Greig challenges us in this:

> "Just as Jesus had spent his time at parties, among the crowds, engaging with the disreputable and apparently non-religious, so today he seems surprisingly comfortable among the crowds of party-goers, the non-religious pilgrims of our time. Perhaps he longs for us to vacate our buildings from time to time, to turn our temples into tabernacles, to become like him, the Friend of Sinners...

Could it be that the Holy Spirit is weary of attending our meetings, and hungers for our presence at his? Perhaps he's dreaming up a thousand new meeting places, where new sounds and sights burn the eyes and hurt the heart!... Maybe this is a new day in which the fullness of God awaits us in the streets and clubs and pubs. But will we hear the Holy Spirit saying, 'Come, holy people?' He waits with Jesus in the darkness until we come, and yet we wonder why maybe he didn't show up the way we hoped at some of our grand events."[27]

A few other thoughts about how to do this:

First, you need to **meet people** who are not believers. That seems self-evident, doesn't it? And yet, to be honest, many of us stumble right here at this crucial juncture. Consider Jesus. He was so good at meeting lost people! But it wasn't accidental. He didn't seem to just wait for it to happen, but was always alert and watchful. "For the Son of Man came to seek and to save the lost." (Luke 19:10). *Seek*. That is not a passive word. It is active. Initiating. Proactive. How did Jesus seek? He was friendly. He went places where lost people might be. He was kind and friendly to folk we might not like or approve of. In fact, He got in trouble for this with the religious leaders, but He didn't seem too concerned about that.

Where can you seek for the lost, both in your daily life, and while doing missions or outreach?

Second, you need to **be authentically spiritual**. In other words, be who you *really* are, wherever you are. If you pray or talk about Jesus or read the Bible in churchy settings,

---

[27] Pete Greig and Dave Roberts, *Red Moon Rising* (Colorado Springs: David C Cook, 2015), pgs 226-227.

do the same in other places. The more openly spiritual you are in diverse settings, the more spiritually hungry people will be attracted to you. The Father is bringing them, pointing them out, making connections. Honestly, this one is hard for me. I tend to think I need to be less obvious so that people will receive me. But this is simply not true. For one, it's not about whether people receive me or not, it's about them receiving Jesus. What good is it for people to like me or think I'm a nice guy apart from Jesus? Friendship with me never changed anyone's heart, and it's simply not going to. But friendship with Jesus! That is another thing altogether. Secondly, I'm looking for the spiritually hungry. How will they know to express their hunger if they don't know I am His?

Third, *open the scriptures*. Once you have identified the spiritually hungry, introduce them to the Word of God. Better than giving them some passages to read on their own, invite them to read with you. This will give you an opportunity to demonstrate how to read the Bible for life-changing transformation. Depending on the background of the person, and their prior knowledge of the Bible, have a few passages in mind that would be good to begin with. As you read aloud with the person, ask questions such as, "What is the writer intending to say here?" "What does this teach us about the character of God? About ourselves?" This process will help the person to read the scriptures with expectation and discernment. It is important -- vitally important -- to move on to a question such as, "How will you obey this scripture in the coming days?" Or, "How will you respond to this?" Remember, the goal of discipleship is obedience to the commands of Jesus, not mere knowledge of them (see Matt 7:24-27 and 28:20). This is so essential! Please don't miss it.

Finally, ask, "Who can you share this truth with in the coming week?" This helps the new disciple to understand that our faith is meant to be shared with other.

Fourth, *invite into Christian community*. As soon as you can, help your friend to join with others for the purposes of growing in Jesus, encouraging one another, and making the Gospel known to others. You don't even need to wait for a profession of faith in order to do this. In fact, gathering with believers who are sincerely seeking Jesus together will help the person make this step. Initially, this may be a few others that you get together with who are studying the Bible together. It may be a full-fledged church or small group within a church. In any case, it is vital for seekers and new disciples to be welcomed into Christian fellowship.

Perhaps it should go without saying -- but it's usually best to articulate it anyway -- that all of this is immersed in prayer. We've discussed this in previous chapters, but it is absolutely essential. Pray for open doors to meet new people. Pray as you seek to genuinely share your faith. Pray for the Lord to connect you with the spiritually hungry. Pray as you begin diving into the scriptures together. Pray as people deliberate putting their trust in Jesus. Pray that Christ be formed in the new disciples, and that they integrate into the people of God. Pray by pouring out your heart to the Father. Pray by listening to the voice of the Spirit. Pray with others, and pray alone. Pray each day. Pray while you walk and while you work and while you play. Pray at appointed times and throughout the day. Pray without ceasing.

"The Kingdom is to be in the midst of your enemies. And he who will not suffer this does not want to be of the

Kingdom of Christ; he wants to be among friends, to sit among roses and lilies, not with the bad people but the devout people. O you blasphemers and betrayers of Christ! If Christ had done what you are doing who would ever have been spared?" (Martin Luther)[28]

---

[28] Quoted in Dietrich Bonhoeffer, *Life Together* (London: SCM Press Tr. John W. Doberstein), p 7.

31 WHAT ABOUT YOUR LIFE?

Taking the Gospel to the nations is worth a few weeks of your summer. Reaching your city with the love of the Father is worth a few hours a week. That is good. I have a really important question for you: Is it worth more than that?

Have you ever considered devoting all of your life to this work? Could you give your best years to a nation in desperate need of the Gospel? Would you consider laying down your life for an inner city community here in the States? If you haven't, why not? If you have, what are you concluding?

The great 19th century preacher, Charles Spurgeon, shared this with his students:

"I plead this day for those who cannot plead for themselves, namely, the great outlying masses of the heathen world. Our existing pulpits are tolerably well supplied, but we need men who will build on new foundations. Who will do this? Are we, as a company of faithful men, clear in our consciences about the heathen? Millions have never heard the name of Jesus. Hundreds of millions have seen a missionary only once in their lives, and know nothing of our King. Shall we let them perish? Can we go to our beds and sleep while China, India, Japan, and other nations are being damned? Are we clear of their

179

blood? Have they no claim upon us? We ought to put it on this footing -- not, 'Can I prove that I *ought* to go?' but 'Can I prove that I *ought not* to go?' When a man can prove honestly that he ought not to go, then he is clear, but not else. What answer do you give, my brethren? I put it to you man by man. I am not raising a question among you that I have not honestly put to myself...[29]

A century or so later, Keith Green echoed this same message in song:

Jesus commands us to go,
But we go the other way.
So he carries the burden alone,
While his children are busy at play,
Feeling so called to stay...

Jesus commands us to go,
It should be the exception if we stay.
It's no wonder we're moving so slow,
When his church refuses to obey,
Feeling so called to stay.[30]

What do we do with that? Is "reaching the world for Christ" something we do when it's convenient? When it fits into our plans and our timetables? As long as we can find time after the important things are covered -- like our work and school and fun and family? Or are we compelled to consider scrapping everything else and pursuing this mission with our entire lives? Yes, it is risky. I know, you have to think about

[29] Charles Spurgeon, *Lectures to My Students* (Zondervan), pg 211.
[30] Keith Green, "Jesus Commands Us to Go," from the album *Jesus Commands Us to Go,* 1984.

money and career and family and... But, having thought about those things, can you offer them to Jesus because He is worth it all, and more?

Can you extend the kingdom and make disciples in business or education or politics or medicine or some other vocation here in the States? Of course! We need people for that, and it may well be that such is your calling. Pursue it with all the zeal and love and grace that He supplies for you.

But can we consider those to whom no one is going, or only very few? Can we seriously think about those locked in the horrible bondage of false religion with nobody there to set them free? Hindus in India. Muslims in the Middle East. Buddhists in Myanmar. What about the refugees, fleeing for their lives, having lost everything? In Spurgeon's words, "Have they no claim upon us?" What about even the poor and homeless and mentally ill in our own cities? Who will lay down their lives for these?

> "When he saw the crowds, he had compassion on them, because they were harassed and helpless, like sheep without a shepherd. Then he said to his disciples, 'The harvest is plentiful but the workers are few. Ask the Lord of the harvest, therefore, to send out workers into his harvest field.'" -- Matthew 9:36-38

Once you have experienced what you have, and seen what you have seen, you have a responsibility. Knowledge is dangerous. You cannot un-know what God's mercy has allowed you to discover through your outreach and mission experiences. Very likely, at some point during your service you have had the thought, "This isn't right! This poverty right here in my city, the lost-ness of these people who are so precious and dear to the Father, the lack of missionaries in this nation, the camp full of refugees that nobody wants." And in your conviction that this isn't right, perhaps you've become convinced that someone ought to do something. Maybe you, like Jesus, have looked out on the pain and brokenness and lostness and hopelessness and felt compassion. And maybe that compassion has led you to pray. And maybe, just maybe, the Father has an answer to that prayer. And perhaps that answer is you.

Again, I am not suggesting that each one of you is called to go this route. But I am suggesting that you are responsible to offer yourself to the Father. To lay down your plans and ambitions, your hopes and your dreams. To even put on the altar the things you were convinced of. And just to simply say, like Isaiah the prophet, "Here am I. Send me." (Isaiah 6:8).

Don't do it lightly. Don't do it if you don't mean it. Count the cost. But take some time away, and surrender your future again to Jesus. Allow Him to disrupt your plans and derail your life. It's His right. He is Lord and Master. And, ultimately, it will be your joy. There will be heartaches and sacrifices and loss. Fears and deprivations and dangers. There will be discomfort and there will be loneliness and there will be pain. But He will be your joy, and you will discover that He is worth it all.

I'm convinced that the Lord is still surveying His people - - His blessed and comfortable and beautiful people, and asking that question, "Whom shall I send? And who will go for us?" (Isaiah 6:8). Can you hear Him? How will you respond?

"I have hitherto lived to little purpose, more like a clod than a servant of God; now let me burn out for God."[31]

— Henry Martyn

---

[31] George Smith, *Henry Martyn: Saint and Scholar* (London: The Religious Tract Society, 1892) in *7 Classic Missionary Biographies* (ClassicChristian eBooks), Location 17593.

NOW GO DO STUFF

Jesus is worth your life. I hope you hear Him calling you to a way of living that is radically counter-cultural. I believe He is searching for a people who will move beyond shallow spirituality and self-focused religion into the wild and beautiful regions of the Kingdom of God. I hear Him calling for a generation who will live not for the emptiness of self-fulfillment but for the fullness of sacrificing all for the Father. If this is the longing of your soul, you are in for quite a ride. There will be tremendous challenges and obstacles in the way, but the grace and power of Jesus will be with you.

I hope you have experienced the conviction of the Holy Spirit as you've read this. But conviction is not the goal. You've got to do something about it. This is a call to action.

> "Do not merely listen to the word, and so deceive yourselves. Do what it says."
>
> — James 1:22

For further encouragement, I'd like to recommend a few books — mostly stories of the lives and ministries of other fully-abandoned Jesus followers. Do whatever you can to continually feed the passion for Jesus and His work. Reading these books will help. See my suggested bibliography on the following pages.

Finally, I'd love to hear from you. If anything in these devotionals has stirred you or inspired questions, let me know. I'd especially be grateful to hear what you are doing as a result of what you've heard the Lord speak to you. You can reach me at tway@tulsaboilerroom.com.

SUGGESTED BIBLIOGRAPHY

Biography. The books that have the most lasting impact on me are generally biographies. Here are some of the best I've come across. The first five in this list especially are pure gold.

Hudson Taylor's Spiritual Secret by Dr and Mrs Howard Taylor

Amy Carmichael of Dohnavur by Frank Houghton

And the Word Came With Power by Joanne Shetler

Living on the Devil's Doorstep by Floyd McClung

Red Moon Rising by Pete Greig

C.T. Studd: Cricketer and Pioneer by Norman Grubb

Life of William Carey by George Smith

The Life and Diary of David Brainerd by David Brainerd and
     Jonathan Edwards

Is That Really You God? by Loren Cunningham

Irresistible Revolution by Shane Claiborne

Through Gates of Splendor by Elizabeth Elliot

My favorite books on **Prayer**:

God on Mute by Pete Greig

With Christ in the School of Prayer by Andrew Murray

Power Through Prayer by E.M. Bounds

Practicing His Presence by Brother Lawrence and Frank Laubach

Celebration of Discipline by Richard Foster

And some general favorites on *Mission*, *Discipleship*, and *Ministry to the Poor*

You See Bones, I See an Army by Floyd McClung

The Vision and the Vow by Pete Greig

Saturate by Jeff Vanderstelt

Missionary Methods: St Paul's or Ours? By Roland Allen

Punk Monk by Andy Freeman

When Helping Hurts by Brian Fikkert and Steve Corbett

The Cost of Discipleship by Dietrich Bonhoeffer

Different by Brian Sanders and Mike Patz

You and Me Forever by Francis and Lisa Chan

Miraculous Movements by Jerry Trousdale

The Ragamuffin Gospel by Brennan Manning

Language Learning is Communication is Ministry by Thomas & Elizabeth Brewster

Ask A Missionary by John McVay

Absolute Surrender by Andrew Murray

ABOUT THE TULSA BOILER ROOM

The Tulsa Boiler Room is a church of churches. It is a Jesus-centered family on His mission together. Our calling is to make disciples through prayer, spiritual family, and intentional outreach. We seek to demonstrate the love and compassion of the Father to the poor and marginalized of our city. Our central activity is prayer, and our posture is availability and vulnerability. We actively seek to equip and send out workers for the Father's harvest. We meet in family-style "simple churches" in homes during the week, and all come together on Sundays to celebrate, be equipped in the Word, welcome the stranger, and enjoy fellowship.

For more information about the Tulsa Boiler Room, go to www.tulsaboilerroom.com or email tulsaboiler@gmail.com.

ABOUT THE MERCHANT AND THURSDAY NIGHT LIGHT

Thursday Night Light is a weekly outreach to the homeless of Tulsa. We set up picnic tables in a parking lot downtown and enjoy a meal with whoever comes. Various businesses, churches, small groups, and families provide the meal each week. It's a simple way of demonstrating the Father's love and initiating relationships with the poor. For more information, find us on Facebook.

facebook.com/ThursdayNightLight

The Merchant is a building that serves as a prayer room and hospitality space for the poor, led by our good friends Paul and Debbie Schmidt. We give away clothing and offer a safe place to come in from the weather. It's a place to rest, enjoy a cup of coffee, receive prayer, engage in conversation, and receive information about networking with other services. It is an available place for people to come meet with the Father in a creative space for prayer.

For more information, look at www.themerchanttulsa.com, or follow us on Facebook: facebook.com/TheMerchantTulsa

THE MUSTARD SEED EXPERIENCE

The Mustard Seed experience is an internship being developed with the Tulsa Boiler Room and the Merchant. It offers an opportunity to learn while engaging in mission in the context of spiritual family. For more information, check out www.tulsaboilerroom.com/mustardseed or write to:
tulsaboiler@gmail.com.

ABOUT THE AUTHOR

Tim Way has been married to Jill for twenty-five years, and they have five children. Together they served as missionaries in Uganda for nine years, and continue to be actively involved in ministry in that beautiful country. Currently Tim helps to pastor the Tulsa Boiler Room and is part of the leadership team for Thursday Night Light and the Merchant. He is involved in multiple avenues of equipping leaders and ministers of the Gospel, both in the US and internationally. He has a Masters Degree in Missions from Oral Roberts University, and is a certified leader in the Antioch School of Church Planting and Leadership Development.